"Tom Scirghi, SJ, writes in the language of a good preacher—direct, informative, clear, personal, and with an awareness of his audience. *Longing to See Your Face* addresses the theology, spirituality, and practicalities of good preaching. While primarily addressed to the ordained preacher, this book will appeal to the increasing numbers of ecclesial lay ministers who preach outside the eucharistic assembly, as well as those who faithfully listen to homilies."

— Jude Siciliano, OP, preacher and instructor in homiletics

"*Longing to See Your Face* is designed for today's preacher, ordained or lay, experienced or just beginning. I commend this work for its fresh theology of preaching and its clear and comprehensive method of preparation, writing, editing, embodiment, and performance. A fine addition to the preaching library."

— Thomas A. Kane, CSP
Boston College School of Theology and Ministry (retired)

Longing to See Your Face

Preaching in a Secular Age

Thomas J. Scirghi, SJ

LITURGICAL PRESS
Collegeville, Minnesota

www.litpress.org

Library of Congress Cataloging-in-Publication Data

Names: Scirghi, Thomas J., author.
Title: Longing to see your face : preaching in a secular age / Thomas J. Scirghi, S.J.
Description: Collegeville, Minnesota : Liturgical Press, 2017.
Identifiers: LCCN 2016037242 (print) | LCCN 2017002350 (ebook) |
    ISBN 9780814637159 | ISBN 9780814637401 (ebook)
Subjects: LCSH: Preaching.
Classification: LCC BV4222 .S35 2017 (print) | LCC BV4222 (ebook) | DDC 251—dc23
LC record available at https://lccn.loc.gov/2016037242

Contents

preach to move hearts —
to elicit consolation.

INTRODUCTION

"Lord, This Is the People That Longs to See Your Face"

Preaching is the act of talking to people about Jesus Christ. Granted, this explanation is terribly simple. But isn't this the role of the preacher, essentially? The preacher speaks to a specific group of people within a particular context. The preacher may speak to the congregation of a parish, or the students in campus ministry of a college or high school, or the residents of a nursing home, or the children of a parish grammar school. And the preacher tells the story of Jesus Christ who is the Son of God and the Savior of the world. This should seem obvious, but how many homilies have we heard that barely mention the name of Jesus Christ? Preaching will test the faith of a preacher who regularly must answer the question, "Who is Jesus Christ?" The preacher stands between the Lord, who has called the preacher to proclaim the word, and the assembly, who longs to see the Lord. This is one way to think of the congregation: the people that longs to see the face of the Lord.

On All Saints' Day, every year, the church chants the first three stanzas of Psalm 24.

> R℣. **Lord, this is the people that longs to see your face.**
>
> The LORD's are the earth and its fullness;
> the world and those who dwell in it.
> For he founded it upon the seas
> and established it upon the rivers.
> Who can ascend the mountain of the LORD?
> or who may stand in his holy place?

1

On whose hands are sinless, whose heart is clean,
> who desires not what is vain.
He shall receive a blessing from the LORD,
> a reward from God his savior.
Such is the race that seeks him,
> that seeks the face of the God of Jacob.

While we repeat the refrain in good faith, we may pause to ask, but how can this be? This plea seems to contradict the experience of Moses at the burning bush when God warned him, "You cannot see my face; for no one shall see me and live" (Exod 33:20). Moses was permitted to see only the back of the Lord. The sight of God would be insufferable to him and to humans. It is a light so brilliant it would be blinding, like staring at the sun during an eclipse. God who is so "other"—who transcends humanity—stands in inaccessible light.

So how can the psalmist announce to almighty God that this people longs to see his face? This announcement is echoed by Jesus at the Sermon on the Mount, "Blessed are the pure in heart, for they will see God" (Matt 5:3-10). Blessed are the pure in heart, that is, blessed are those who are free from all selfish intentions and from self-seeking desires. It seems that both the psalmist and Jesus invite their followers to enter the world of God's reign. They invoke a new order. Both invert the value of the world and promise that the people may indeed see God. But the people must prepare themselves. They must come before the Lord with clean hands and a pure heart. God's dwelling is holy and all who enter it should be holy as well.

Some Scripture scholars comment that Psalm 24 was sung as a liturgical hymn. It may have been used in an entrance procession into the sanctuary. It opens with a profession of faith, acknowledging the Lord as the Creator of the universe. It then asks who shall be admitted to the temple. Those who do enter will receive blessings from the Lord. Those who enter God's reign have been shaped by their loyalty to God. They recognize God as the Creator of all. The prescription for clean hands and pure heart is no mere call for ritual purity. Rather, it questions where we stand in relation with God. Those with pure hearts see, like the psalmist, that "The earth is the LORD's and all that is in it." Almighty God, who reigned in chaos for creation, still rules over the world.

Today, the preacher, standing in the sanctuary, serves as the mediator between the Lord and the people. The preacher views the people in their relationship with God. The people ask how they may be made ready to meet the Lord. Preaching is about preparing the faithful to meet the Lord. The ordained preacher emerges from the faithful and is authorized to lead them in seeking the face of God.

Preaching is a most important work of the priest. The church declared at the Second Vatican Council, "For since nobody can be saved who has not first believed, it is the first task of priests as co-workers of the bishops to preach the Gospel of God to all. In this way they carry out the Lord's command, 'Go into all the world and preach the Gospel to every creature' (Mk 16:15)" (*Presbyterorum Ordinis* [Decree on the Ministry and Life of Priests], 4).[1] The priest's duty to preach follows from the command of Jesus to his disciples. The Catholic Church realizes the power of the word, when proclaimed from the pulpit, to reveal the presence of God in our midst. We receive the Body and Blood of Christ with the Eucharist; we receive the word of God with the proclamation of the Scripture. To illustrate this, consider the fourfold presence of God as described in *Sacrosanctum Concilium* (The Constitution on the Sacred Liturgy). In the celebration of the Eucharist, Christ is present in the person of the minister, in the eucharistic species, in the assembly of the faithful, and "He is present in his word since it is he himself who speaks when the holy scriptures are read in church" (7).

At this point, some readers may comment, "But don't we know this already?" Maybe so. But experience has shown that some welcome the chance to hear this once again, while others may hear it for the first time. As I have held classes in preaching across the United States, as well as in Asia, Africa, and Australia, two concerns continue to surface. One is theoretical and asks, "Why do we preach? What is the purpose of preaching?" The other is practical, asking for new strategies in preparation and helpful points for presenting the homily. I think of these classes, whether with seminarians or seasoned preachers, priests, deacons, and laity, as an exercise in finding one's voice. The instructor cannot tell the students how to preach so much as free them to articulate an ancient message for a modern audience. There is also truth to the adage that "preaching is caught rather than taught." This is to say that learning to preach is similar to learning an art or a sport. We may learn much from manuals and mentors, but eventually we must adapt the instruction and experience to our own ability.

With this in mind, the book begins with a discussion of the purpose of preaching. It offers a theological sounding on proclamation, and takes up several descriptions of the role of the preacher in relation to the congregation. It also addresses some current theological issues for the contemporary preacher. The second part of the book takes up the practical matter of preparing to preach. It proposes a method of preparation by following a pattern of, what I call, the four Rs: reflect, research, write, and rehearse. The third part focuses on two specific sacramental celebrations, namely, the funeral and the wedding. In workshops on preaching, priests and deacons often ask for special instruction on these two sacraments.

The audience for the book is threefold. First, it is written for ordained preachers—bishops, priests, deacons, and seminarians soon to be ordained. It is hoped that it will serve this audience either as a primer or a refresher manual. Second, it is written for ecclesial lay ministers, a growing office in the Catholic Church. These ministers are called upon to preach for funeral vigils, liturgies with children, Sunday eucharistic worship when a priest is not available, and on spiritual retreats. Through their study of the Christian tradition and their experience in ministry, they bear a message from the Lord for the people of God. Also, it should be noted that, while the book is written within a Roman Catholic context, it is hoped that the sections on purpose and preparation will be found relevant to all Christian preachers. Third, the book is written for the faithful who sit and listen faithfully to homilies Sunday after Sunday, on weekdays as well. They spend time on an annual retreat; they celebrate weddings, baptisms, and funerals with family and friends. Through all of this they hope to hear a word of encouragement from the Lord. It is hoped that the contents here may help the congregation to appreciate more of what is spoken from the pulpit and how it is presented. Perhaps it will provide criteria for the congregation so that they may offer constructive feedback to their preachers. There is no shortage of worshipers wishing to comment on preaching—what they admire about their preachers and what they find unsatisfying. And the preachers come to understand their pastoral role, standing before these people, the ones longing to see the face of God.

PART I

Is Anyone Listening?

Is anyone listening? I wondered this one day on a flight from Los Angeles to Las Vegas. It was my regular visit for a diocesan weekend workshop on preaching. I have come to enjoy these occasional weekends, working with deacons and lay ministers, preparing them to evangelize: to spread the good news and to become heralds of the word of God. At the risk of sounding "over the top," isn't this the purpose of preaching? A course in preaching is more than a public speaking course. The message we preach gives us words to live by and, at times, to die for.

These ideas streamed through my mind as the airplane was about to take off. The flight attendant interrupted my thoughts, though, with the required safety announcement. For those who fly regularly, the instructions are familiar: how to buckle your seatbelt, where to find the safety exits, how the oxygen masks will fall from the overhead compartment in case of low cabin pressure, that there's a life vest stowed under your seat to be used in the case of a water landing, and absolutely no smoking on board the aircraft . . . now, relax and enjoy the flight. I suppose it's the teacher in me that wants to respect the speaker at the front of the room, so I gave my attention to him. As I looked around, though, I saw most of the passengers ignoring him. Some had their heads buried in books or magazines, or their ears covered with earphones. Others had fallen asleep. I listened to the attendant recite from memory the airline's instructions in a dutiful manner. Some of us chuckled when he explained the instruction of what to do in case of an emergency water landing. In flying from Los Angeles to Las Vegas the land below is almost all desert. The only water landing would occur if we landed in someone's backyard pool! But this is part of the regular instruction and so it must be announced.

The attendant fulfilled an obligation, but was anybody listening? After all, we passengers really do not expect anything to go wrong. Hopefully the most difficult part of the trip was dealing with security. We just want this plane to get up into the air and get us to our destination. These instructions really do not matter much. We respect that the attendant has a job to do and that he has to make his speech, but the passengers do not have to listen. It then occurred to me: Is this what preachers face on any given Sunday? Given that I was flying to a preacher's workshop, I saw the flight attendant standing like a preacher before a congregation.

The preacher is, to say the least, fulfilling an obligation. The Sunday celebration of the Eucharist requires a homily. According to the *General Instruction of the Roman Missal*, "On Sundays and Holydays of Obligation there is to be a Homily at every Mass that is celebrated with the people attending, and it may not be omitted without a grave reason" (66). And so the preacher speaks to us about the good news of Jesus Christ. But how often will the congregation receive this message like the airline passengers? Sometimes a congregation may act as if they do not expect to hear anything new or different. They act as if it really doesn't matter. And sometimes a preacher can act as if he does not expect his words to make a difference. We all march through the routine of worship. Fred Craddock, a New Testament scholar and a fine preacher, compared some preachers to swimming coaches who bark instructions to their athletes from the side of the pool, but do not expect anyone to jump into the water.

Why does preaching matter? In short, because preaching provides an opportunity to encounter Christ. In the words of Pope Benedict, in his address to the bishops' synod on the New Evangelization, "Being Christian is not the result of an ethical choice or a lofty idea, but the encounter with an event, a person which gives life a new horizon and a decisive direction."[1] In this way preaching is sacramental. Each of the sacraments provides the faithful with a special opportunity to meet the living Lord. The word of God mediated through the church's minister comes alive for us in new ways. We should explore this topic in greater depth and ask, what is the purpose of preaching? To answer this question, we will discuss three authors: a bishop of the early Middle Ages, a contemporary theologian, and an evangelist. Each one offers us a way to appreciate the importance of evangelization.

CHAPTER ONE

Why Do We Preach?
The Purpose of Preaching

Go into all the world and proclaim the good news to the whole creation.

—Mark 16:15

Saint Augustine gives us a good description of preaching. It is commonly known that Augustine was well poised to advise preachers. He studied rhetoric in Milan and became a master in the art of persuasive speech. After his conversion to Christianity he used the tools of rhetoric to promote the Gospel. In his book *On Christian Doctrine* (part IV), the bishop of Hippo provides what may be the first manual on preaching. Referring to the "Orations" of Cicero, Augustine writes, "A certain eloquent man said, and said truly, that he who is eloquent should speak in such a way that he teaches, delights, and moves. . . . To teach is a necessity, to please is a sweetness, to persuade is a victory" (Orations 21.69). An eloquent speech should teach, delight, and move. Let's say a word about each of these.

For Augustine, to *teach* while preaching means to instruct on matters of Scripture and the teaching of the church. Good preaching helps to expand and deepen our understanding of the Bible and the tradition so that we grow as members of the baptized community. As Christians we ask ourselves, What does it mean to be a Christian today? How do I express my faith in Jesus Christ who is the Son of God and the Savior of humanity? To be clear, to teach, in this sense, does not mean to turn the ambo into a professor's podium. The preacher is not supposed to deliver a lecture on the Scripture or on a moral concern of the day. Rather, the people should hear an old story in a new way and understand how to adapt it to their lives. Moreover, the preacher may want to enlighten the congregation on an appropriate teaching of the church. This is how the preacher "teaches."

To *delight* means to inspire. The word is derived from the Latin root *inspirare,* meaning to breathe upon or into. Recall after the resurrection when Jesus greeted the disciples by saying "Peace be with you," and breathed the Holy Spirit upon them (John 20:21-22). The disciples knew they were in the presence of the Lord. In a similar vein, Augustine prays, "Lord, my faith calls upon you, that faith which you have given to me, which you have breathed into me by the incarnation of your Son and through the ministry of your preacher" (*Confessions* 1.1.1). Sacramental preaching should provide an opportunity for the listeners to encounter the risen Lord and to breathe in the Spirit of the Lord. It should be clear that, by "delight," Augustine did not mean for the preacher to entertain. The pulpit is not the place for telling jokes or spinning folktales. Instead the congregation should hear the Scripture in a new way, one that speaks to their hearts, and provides the listeners with an opportunity to meet the Lord in their own lives. It is when we hear a person say, "Preacher, it is as if you were talking to me!"—this person felt inspired.

To *move* means to leave the listeners wanting to respond to the message and offering a means by which they may respond. It is as if they say, "What can I do now?" Jesus Christ is no mere celebrity from whom we ask an autograph and a selfie, and then leave him. Meeting the Lord requires a response from us. As we listen to him in the proclaimed word, perhaps we hear a personal call and are moved to more fervent prayer, or to more generous service, or to a change in our lifestyle. Now that we have heard the word of God, what difference will it make in our lives? We find a good example of this "movement" with Peter preaching at Pentecost. Recall the scene on that feast day in Jerusalem. At first we see Peter in the Upper Room, cowering with the crowd of apostles, all of them fearing for their lives. And with good reason. They worried that they would be charged with being associates of Jesus and meet the same fate on Calvary. Then the Holy Spirit intruded and inspired them all. In a remarkable transition Peter courageously stepped onto the balcony and preached to the crowd below. He told them of how Jesus of Nazareth was the Messiah of whom the prophets spoke. He argued that Jesus had been unfairly sentenced to death and suffered brutally. Nevertheless it was because of his death and resurrection that humanity has been forgiven for its sinfulness. He must have moved them with his speech, for as St. Luke reports,

> When they heard this, they were cut to the heart and said to Peter and to the other apostles, 'Brothers, what should we do?' Peter said to them, 'Repent, and be baptized every one of you in the name of Jesus Christ so that your sins may be forgiven; and you will receive the gift of the Holy Spirit.'. . . So those who welcomed his message were baptized, and that day about three thousand persons were added. They devoted themselves to the apostles' teaching and fellowship, to the breaking of bread and the prayers. (Acts 2:37-38, 41-42)

Preaching should move the listeners so that, as the psalmist says, "O that today you would listen to his voice! / Do not harden your hearts" (Ps 95:7-8).

Teach, delight, and move. Augustine borrowed this scheme from classical rhetoric and applied it to preaching. We can imagine, then, that after Bishop Augustine preached in his cathedral at Hippo, he would hope to hear some members of the congregation say, "Good sermon, bishop. I learned something new today. You gave me an insight into the Scripture. Also, the way you presented your message challenged me; it was as if you were talking specifically to me. And now I know what I must do to keep faith with the Lord." This ancient rhetorical scheme still provides a framework for the purpose of preaching.

For a more contemporary description of the purpose of preaching we might think of it as "naming grace." This idea comes from the book *Naming Grace: Preaching and the Sacramental Imagination*, by Sr. Mary Catherine Hilkert. A member of the Dominican Order, Sr. Hilkert is professor of theology at Notre Dame University. She describes preaching as the art of naming grace in the depths of human experience.[1] Let's look at two terms here: "grace" and "the depths of human experience."

"Grace," very simply, refers to the presence of God. According to the *Catechism of the Catholic Church*, "Grace is *favor*, the *free and undeserved help* that God gives us to respond to his call to become children of God, . . . partakers of the divine nature and of eternal life. Grace is a *participation in the life of God*."[2] Hilkert says that in Christian worship we celebrate the mystery of God's presence here and now (46).

To illustrate the "depths of human experience" Hilkert cites the Scripture story of the apostles Peter and John healing a lame man. This story is found in the Acts of the Apostles, 3:1-26. In this story Peter and John were on their way to the temple for prayer. They passed a man who had been lame from birth. The man asked them for money. Peter told the man that they had neither silver nor gold, but commanded him, "In the name of Jesus Christ of Nazareth, stand up and walk." The man leapt up and walked into the temple with Peter and John, and there gave praise to God. The other people who were milling about recognized the man and were astonished to see him walking. Peter then addressed the crowd. He assured them that it was not the power of the apostles that cured the crippled man. Rather, "the faith that is through Jesus has given him this perfect health in the presence of all of you." After explaining this, Peter went on to chastise the crowd, for, in their ignorance, they put Christ to death. He then told them to "repent therefore, and turn to God so that your sins may be wiped out, so that times of refreshing may come from the presence of the Lord." Hilkert sees Peter as a model for the preacher. He interprets what is happening in the depths of the community's experience and points to the power and the presence of God. In other words, he names grace (45).

Notice the double-edged sword entailed in "naming grace." On the one hand, it is comforting to know that God dwells with us, revealing himself through an act of miraculous healing. On the other hand, we are challenged to respond to God's presence in our midst. We must either accept it or reject it. Peter accuses the crowd of having rejected Christ, sending him to his death. But now they have the opportunity to repent, to convert, or, in his words, to turn again. Think of the Rite of Baptism when Christians renounce the lure of Satan and turn toward the Son of God. The presence of God is not merely an announcement; it is a summons, a call to follow him. Recall the gospel stories where Jesus meets the disciples. He does not simply announce himself, as if he were an itinerant rabbi seeking followers. He commands them: "Follow me, and I will make you fish for people" (Matt 4:19). And they do. Yet, considering the human condition, this is easier said than done. As we plumb the depths of human experience we realize how difficult it is to respond to the word of God. Hilkert cites Richard Lischer, who says, "Any theology that takes the Word of God seriously must reckon with its greatest source of embarrassment: the word must be spoken and received by sinful human beings."[3] In Christian worship we hear sinners preaching to other sinners about the promise of salvation.

Of course it is one thing to hear the story of Peter and John with the lame man and to be astonished by a miracle cure. From the healing action of the apostles we are directed to divine revelation. However, as Hilkert notes, in the contemporary world the experience of God for most people comes in the face of, and in spite of, human suffering (49). The prevalence of human suffering around us raises the old question of theodicy: How do we justify our belief in God, who is all knowing, all powerful, and all good, in the face of such evil? To address this conundrum Hilkert calls on another Dominican, Fr. Edward Schillebeeckx, and his concept of the "contrast experience." According to Schillebeeckx, while the experience of the majority of humanity is that of suffering and the apparent absence of God, a still deeper mystery is revealed by their response to that suffering, namely, a response of protest, hope, and sheer endurance. Human beings are able to cling to life against all odds, and cling to God even when God is silent. That kind of human resistance and hope can be sustained only by a deeper spirit of life, which is the Spirit of God within humanity (52). In short, the contrast experience recognizes the tremendous capacity for hope that pervades the human condition. To experience hopefulness in the midst of suffering will serve to proclaim the presence of God.

For example, after the tragedy of September 11, 2001, many people were left asking, "Where was God in all of this?" Some rushed to defend God in this tragedy. A friend of mine tried to answer the question. She explained to me that while so many people complained of not finding God in the wake of this tragedy, with over three thousand people dead, they failed to notice the number of people who were saved. "This is where God was," she explained triumphantly, "standing with the saved!"

Well, excuse me for sounding cynical but I could not accept this apologia, and I told her so. Her explanation seems to suggest that God saved some of the people but, for some reason, just could not save everyone. It is as if God swung by the devastated area with a rescue boat; however, the vessel was not big enough for all the victims. Only some could be saved. Personally, I do not find this explanation consoling. Instead, I prefer the words of a preacher whom I heard shortly after that day. He reminded the congregation of one image from that fateful day that was still etched in our minds—the image of the first tall tower, an inferno, with flames shooting out from its two sides. The tower and the flames made the shape of a cross. Then, a second airplane crossed in front of the first tower. It looked like a spear piercing the side of the cross. The preacher then said, "There was Christ—with the dying."

Again, the purpose of preaching is to name grace, that is, to locate Christ's presence here and now. We need to be wary, though, of finding Christ solely with the success stories, for example, of locating the Lord with those who have been cured of cancer, or with those who have found what they were looking for, be it a job, a home, or a partner with whom they will share their lives. God dwells with them certainly, and we should be grateful for our good fortune. However, an overemphasis on finding God with the success stories may make some wonder if God has abandoned them—if they are not cured of cancer, or if they did not find what they were looking for. God dwells also with the failures and the losers. Their loss may be transformed into a means of finding the Lord, and this becomes a sign of grace.

Furthermore, Christians are hopeful rather than merely optimistic. Optimism is good, certainly. It is good to be looking on the bright side of life, to see the light at the end of the tunnel, or to judge the glass to be half full rather than half empty. All of this is good. But Christian hope goes deeper. Guided by hope we trust that, together with God, we will thrive. It is when you cannot find a bright side to life, but you still hope. (As we read in the Letter to the Hebrews, "Now faith is the assurance of things hoped for, the conviction of things not seen" [11:1].) It is when you cannot see the light at the end of the tunnel, but you still hope. (Remember the words of Psalm 139, "even the darkness is not dark to you; / the night is as bright as the day, / for darkness is as light to you" [v. 12].) It is when the glass is neither half full nor half empty; it is just empty and there is nothing left. (Remember Jesus' first miracle, during the wedding at Cana, when the surprised steward exclaimed, "But you have kept the good wine until now"! [John 2:1-11].) Hopefulness—the disposition of remaining hopeful—is the crux of Christianity. When we think it is over, that all is lost, and we are shrouded in darkness, that is the time when God gives us more, and better than we could have imagined.

So the preacher names grace—the presence of Christ in our midst—in the successes as well as in the failures. In the attempt to name grace we describe how Christ is present to us here and now. In every event of our lives, from funeral to festival, and through the routine of daily life, Christ stands with us and speaks to us; can we hear him? In Hilkert's words, "To tell the human story in its depth, as Jesus did, is to point to the mystery of God at the heart of human existence, to 'name grace'" (53).

Here is one final note on the purpose of preaching, taken from the evangelist St. Luke. We can learn a lesson from the story of the two disciples on the road to Emmaus (Luke 24:13-35). In this story we hear one of the disciples ask, "Were not our hearts burning . . . while he was opening the scriptures to us?" Recall how, along the way to the town of Emmaus, the two disciples encountered a stranger. The recent events in Jerusalem had worried them. They had heard an outrageous rumor that Jesus of Nazareth had risen from death. It was outrageous because no one had ever risen from the dead in all of history, as far as they knew. Yet, who would make up such a story? But if it were true, their lives would be changed forever. As disciples, they would not be able to return to their ordinary way of life; they would live their lives on mission. And so they wandered in a quandary.

Along the way they met a stranger. He chided them for their confusion: "How slow of heart [you are] to believe." Then the stranger rehearsed salvation history for them, from the patriarchs through the prophets to the present, enabling them to see that the one who was crucified was the one of whom was prophesied. The disciples may have seen a connection between Jesus and the Messiah, but they still could not see the stranger for who he was, at least not until they would break bread together. Later on, they followed the Jewish custom of hospitality, inviting him to spend the evening with them. As they sat down for dinner they also invited him to pronounce the blessing. Following the Jewish practice he took a piece of bread, gave thanks to God for the food they were about to eat, and broke it in order to share it. Suddenly there was a flash of recognition: Indeed, he is the one of whom the prophets spoke and who was glorified by God. I imagine the two disciples sitting there stunned, staring in awe at the broken bread while their guest had vanished.

Then one of them spoke up, "Were not our hearts burning . . . while he was opening the scriptures to us?" Let us pause and consider the power of this word "opening." Sometimes it has been translated as "explaining," suggesting a didactic approach to the Scriptures, almost like a classroom setting where a teacher might explain a passage of literature. But a closer look reveals a more vibrant message. In this passage, Luke the evangelist uses the Greek word *dianoigo,* meaning "to open." The word means more than simply opening a book or a bottle of wine. It is interesting to note that there is one other place in the gospel where Luke uses this same word. We find it in the account of the presentation of Jesus in the temple: "[A]s it is written in the law of the Lord, 'Every male that *opens* the womb shall be consecrated to the Lord'" (Luke 2:23, NABRE).

This is a most dramatic opening. The firstborn child, who is received into a loving household, has a way of rejuvenating a family. This child changes the relationships within a family. I can imagine a similar experience for the two disciples—similar in that they were rejuvenated because their relationship with Jesus Christ, and with one another, was renewed. Their faith, which lay dormant since the crucifixion, was now revived. The Scriptures were opened to them and they found themselves within the story. The word of God came alive to them, and consequently they cannot return to life as usual; they now belong with Christ and with the Christian community.

It is ironic that they recognize Christ in the breaking of the bread. For isn't this what happens to them? They are broken like the bread. They are changed; their lives are reoriented; they are broken open so that they may receive the word of God. In fact, we could find a parallel between what Jesus does with the bread and what he does with all his disciples. At the Last Supper, Jesus took bread, blessed it, broke it, and then gave it. In a similar way, Jesus called his disciples. Recall the scene at the Sea of Galilee when Jesus commanded Peter and the others to drop everything and follow him. He called them, they responded, and he "took" them. Later he "blessed" them, thanking his father for them. Later still, he needed to "break" them, that is, to change their way of seeing so that they would come to recognize him as the Son of God. Recall, too, their many moments of doubt and confusion, and Jesus' frustration with them. For example, there was the time when Jesus scolded Peter, telling him, "Get behind me, Satan! You are a stumbling block to me; for you are setting your mind not on divine things but on human things" (Matt 16:23). Peter's way of looking at Jesus needed to be broken so that he could see as Christ sees. Finally, he "gives" them, missioning them to the ends of the earth, instructing them to heal the sick, to forgive sins, to teach and to baptize. As Jesus did with the bread, so he did with his first disciples, and continues to do so, to this day.

Note that the breaking of the bread was a most significant action for the early Christian community. It defined them. Before they were known as "Christians," they were referred to as the people who break bread together. Indeed, they were true "companions" of the Lord and of one another. The word "companion" is derived from the Latin *cum pane*, meaning "with bread." In Jesus' day, companionship was demonstrated by sharing bread.

The two disciples on the road to Emmaus recognized Jesus in the breaking of bread. When Jesus opened the Scripture he did not merely explain a lesson to the disciples. Rather, like a great storyteller, he opened the story so that they would find themselves within it and their lives would be renewed. Good preaching continues to open the Scripture so that the faithful may find themselves within the gospel story once again.

CHAPTER TWO

Words Matter: The Power of the Word

Laugh at ministers all you want, they have the words we
need to hear, the ones the dead have spoken.

—John Updike

As we discuss the purpose of preaching, we need to appreciate
also the power of words. The quote above is taken from John
Updike's novel *Rabbit Is Rich*, the third book in the "Rabbit" series.
In one scene from this story the protagonist, Harry Angstrom,
attends a Christian wedding. Harry takes note of the preacher
who, while small in stature, speaks with a commanding voice. In
Harry's words, the preacher is able to gather the straggling audience into a congregation, "subduing any fear that this ceremony
might be a farce."[1] Indeed, ministers have the words we need to
hear.

Words suffer a bad reputation these days. We hear phrases like
"It's only words," or "That is mere rhetoric," or "Actions speak
louder than words." All this suggests that words hold little importance. So, can we trust the spoken word? Yet, Christians and
Jews inherit the tradition of a living word. Within this tradition,
the spoken word calls creation into being, establishes a covenant
between God and humanity, reconciles relationships among nations, and offers hope in the face of despair.

Emerging from this tradition, the preacher stands before a congregation like the prophet Isaiah standing among the Israelites.

Listen to Isaiah's proclamation: "The Lord GOD has given me / the tongue of a teacher, / that I may know how to sustain / the weary with a word. / Morning by morning he wakens— / wakens my ear / to listen as those who are taught. . . . and I was not rebellious, / I did not turn backward" (Isa 50:4-5). Isaiah spoke to the Israelites who, at this point in their history, were struggling through the exile. Far from home they had grown weary. Weariness is a recurring theme for Isaiah (e.g., 40:29-31; 43:23-24). His people were weary as they wandered through a foreign land. The Israelites wondered if they would ever return home, and they worried that God had abandoned them. However, God sent prophets to his people to encourage them and to bolster their faith. God's word, spoken through the prophet, renewed the Israelites, and many of them remained faithful during their exile.

The word of God held great power for them. For the ancient Hebrews the spoken word meant more than a vocal utterance or a piece of information; rather, something was happening. The Hebrew word *dabar*, meaning "word," signals an event. Remember the story of creation and how the universe came into being when God spoke, "Let there be light," and then called forth into being every living creature (Gen 1:1-31). God continues to speak and we witness an ongoing creation. Listen to another prophecy of Isaiah: "For as the rain and the snow come down from heaven, / and do not return there until they have watered the earth, / making it bring forth and sprout, / giving seed to the sower and bread to the eater, / so shall my word be that goes out from my mouth; / it shall not return to me empty, / but it shall accomplish that which I purpose, / and succeed in the thing for which I sent it" (Isa 55:10-11).

When God speaks, something happens. And the word of God is spoken through prophets and preachers. This is the word that the prophet spoke to rouse a weary nation. Jesus echoed Isaiah when he preached at the synagogue in his hometown of Nazareth. There he proclaimed, "The spirit of the Lord is upon me, / because he has anointed me / to bring good news to the poor. / He has sent me to proclaim release to the captives / and recovery of sight to the blind, / to let the oppressed go free, / to proclaim the year of the Lord's favor" (Luke 4:18-19).

Preachers today speak like Isaiah in the desert and like Jesus in the synagogue. They speak to an assembly weary from "exile," a people feeling estranged even in their own land, whether it is due to political strife, economic hardship, the effects of old age, the scourge of addictive behavior, or young parents struggling to raise children. This is the people longing to see the face of the Lord. This is not to say that the world is an evil place, but that we walk somewhere between the Garden of Eden and the Valley of Gehenna. We are aware of the beauty and goodness around us, yet we are mindful of the presence and power of evil wearing us down. We recognize that the world should not be the way it is. So we welcome the preacher, the one who can speak a rousing word, the word we need to hear. Today's preachers continue the ancient tradition of proclaiming the word of God. They reveal God's presence through the spoken word.

Our words do matter. So we should be wary of expressions that suggest words are insignificant. Some say, "Words are cheap." I beg to differ. Words are not cheap; however, we may cheapen them. We cheapen words through misuse and through vulgarity. We cheapen them when we serve them up like a fast-food meal: quick, inexpensive, and convenient. For those who would say, "Those are just words," consider the following. Picture a labor and delivery room, where a young father assists his wife while she labors, waiting anxiously for their first child's arrival, and finally at the birth, the nurse says, "It's a boy!" Or standing outside an emergency room, a family waits for news of their father who was just rushed to the hospital in serious condition, and a surgeon says to them, sadly, "I'm sorry." Picture a young man on bended knee, proposing to his beloved and he asks, "Will you marry me?" Just words? Think of the speeches that roused a nation in a time of trial. For instance, the movie *The King's Speech* demonstrates the power of the spoken word as George VI, the reluctant king, struggled through his stammer to rouse a weary nation in a time of war, and he galvanized his people, at home and abroad. Just words? Actions may speak louder than words at times, but often words precede the actions, directing people, giving them the courage they need and a way of proceeding. Think of the priest at Mass when he elevates the host and announces, "This is my Body." Or in the confessional when he says to the penitent, "I absolve you from your sins." Or during a funeral, at the gravesite, where he prays, "But the Lord Jesus Christ will change our mortal bodies to be like his in glory, / for he is risen, the firstborn from the dead" (Rite of Committal 219A). Just words?

Here is another commonly heard phrase that demeans speech: "Words cannot express how we feel today." While there are some situations when words elude us, making it difficult to express our feeling or understanding, I would argue that in many situations there are indeed words to fit the occasion. Perhaps, however, we have not found the appropriate phrase. If we trawl through our literary tradition there is a good chance we will find something appropriate and meaningful. Consider the plays of Shakespeare and Sophocles, the poetry of Plath and Poe, the novels of Tolstoy and Twain, the speeches of Churchill and Lincoln, the songs of Sinatra, Sondheim, and Springsteen, the operas of Wagner and Mozart, the philosophies of Aristotle and Ayn Rand, the showings of Julian of Norwich and the writings of Dorothy Day, and, of course, the parables of Jesus. Apologies for this long litany, but we need to emphasize that, before we say that we cannot find the words, or that words cannot express our sentiment, we should ask honestly how thoroughly we have searched for them.

Remember Qoheleth's sage advice: "What has been is what will be, / and what has been done is what will be done; / there is nothing new under the sun" (Eccl 1:9). Have we taken the time to study our culture to find the words that express the hope and joy, or the pain and anxiety, of the moment? This was one strength of Martin Luther King's preaching. He had the ability to express the fear and frustration of his audience. For example, in the beginning of his speech "I Have a Dream," he addressed the frustration that the promises of the Emancipation Proclamation, signed a century ago, have not been realized yet. In his words, "One hundred years later the Negro still is not free . . . the life of the Negro is still badly crippled by the manacles of segregation and the chains of discrimination . . . the Negro lives on a lonely island of poverty in the midst of a vast ocean of material prosperity . . . the Negro is still languished in the corners of American society and finds himself in exile in his own land." King was able to name with graphic imagery the plight of his people. By doing so he helped to lift them out of despair and move them forward, directing them along a path that promised hope, with words drawn from Scripture. "I have a dream that one day every valley shall be exalted, every hill and mountain shall be made low. The rough places will be made plain, and the crooked places will be made straight. And the glory of the Lord shall be revealed, and all flesh shall see it together" (see Luke 3:4-6). Dr. King preached like the prophets of old, speaking truth to power. His words, the fruit of his prayer and experience, uplifted many of his listeners. Clearly he had the words people needed to hear.

CHAPTER THREE

Naming the Unknown God:
Preaching within a Secular Society

How could we sing the LORD's song
in a foreign land?

—Psalm 137:4

Today we see a cultural shift in the way people understand religion. There is much concern, and with good reason, over the rapid rise of "nones," those who do not affiliate with traditional, organized religion. Many nones express a distrust of institutional religion. They are often referred to as "spiritual but not religious," that is to say, they claim to have some form of spirituality, but do not find a home within any particular church. They tend to be either overwhelmed or repelled by church doctrine. And they are part of a rising tide of secularism, a movement that includes those who identify as either atheist or agnostic. This shift is documented in a 2015 study by Pew Research Center titled *America's Changing Religious Landscape: Christians Decline Sharply as Share of Population; Unaffiliated and Other Faiths Continue to Grow*. The question I will ask here is, How can Christian preaching engage nones in conversation about the "object of our worship," Jesus Christ? To answer this let us first take a closer look at the challenge from rising secularism. Second, I believe that St. Paul may help move us toward a solution with his speech at the Areopagus, found in the Acts of the Apostles. Third, "Catholic" preaching has the means to include the journey of nones and secularists, and to move them forward in faith.

The Rise of Nones

First, let us consider the problem. According to the Pew study, in the United States today, approximately 25 percent of people claim to be "nonreligious." Nearly one-third of all millennials, those who were born between 1981 and 1996, consider themselves to be "nones." The movement away from religious affiliation is the fastest growing religious orientation in the country. This movement is fueled, in part, by secularism.

Secularism expresses an emphasis on "rational pragmatism." Phil Zuckerman, in his 2014 book *Living the Secular Life*, explains this position, which reminds us all that human beings are rational creatures, endowed with reason. However, human reason is distinguished from religious belief, as he finds the two to be in mutual opposition. In their criticism of religion, secularists tend to draw a caricature of believers, portraying them as fearful and superstitious, making them gullible for belief in God. They sometimes focus on religious extremists, be they Christians, Jews, or Muslims. The extremists—those who follow their faith blindly and are prone to act violently—become the norm by which all religious people are judged. Secularists seem to presume that people come to religion either out of fear (and they need someone to protect them) or out of ignorance (and they need someone to explain the inexplicable). To their minds, the eternal questions, such as, "Why do bad things happen to good people?" or "What happens to us when we die?" beg for answers for which the gullible will turn to God.

Perhaps preachers need to reflect for a moment and ask, Why do we believe in God? Is it out of fear or out of wonder? Fear or wonder? Personally speaking, the reason I am a Catholic Christian today is due to wonder: to wonder where we come from and where we are going; to marvel at human accomplishments as well as to lament our failings; to believe there is a purpose to our existence, and that the story of Jesus Christ gives meaning to our lives. Let us look, briefly, at these three "wonders."

First of all, some of us wonder about our origins. Here science and religion do not contradict one another. As Pope Francis explains, "The Big Bang theory, which is proposed today as the origin of the world, does not contradict the intervention of a divine creator but depends on it."[1] Is it ironic that the theory was first proposed in the 1920s by George Lemaître, who was a Belgian priest and scholar? Likewise, the theory of evolution makes good sense scientifically, but it still begs the question of how or why the chain of evolution began. Pope Francis comments, "Evolution in nature does not conflict with the notion of Creation, because evolution presupposes the creation of beings who evolve."[2]

Second, we do lament our failings. Here we will focus on our moral failings. Some secularists claim that the only necessary moral code is the "Golden Rule," to do unto others as you would have them do unto you. Zuckerman argues that, as members of a society, we have a moral obligation to help those in need and to refrain from hurting anyone. Now, would any reasonable person disagree with this? Of course, the Golden Rule is a good principle for proper moral conduct, but it is an abstraction. It begs the question of how we may put into practice this principle in our daily life. To live like a good person it can be more effective to follow people rather than rules. The philosopher Aristotle advised, If you want to learn how to be a good person, watch a good person. If we want to know how to live like a good man or woman, we need a model of such a life. Christians have that model in Jesus Christ, and the model is carried on through the saints and through the whole Body of Christ, the church. It is a model of moral living, showing us how we ought to live. Moreover, it is a model for loving others, to devote oneself to another, to sacrifice when necessary, and to find meaning in life through the love of others.

Third, do we believe that our lives have purpose and meaning, and that there is an order to the world? Or do we think that the cycle of life is merely random, and that our lives are governed by chance? Many do accept that the future is ruled by chance. Take the film director Woody Allen, for example. His film *Match Point* tells a story of a life governed by luck. It is a good story and told well on the screen. The meaning is in the metaphor "match point," a tennis term. Allen uses the image of a tennis match, at a point when the ball hits the top of the net and spins upward. A player does not aim for this shot; it happens accidentally; it happens by chance. For a moment, as the ball spins upward, we see that it could go forward, bounce into the opponent's court, and the player will win the point. Or the ball could go backward and the player will lose the point. It is all up to chance. The message the viewer takes away is that our lives are somewhat like a tennis match: so much is determined by chance.

In contrast, Roman Catholics believe that the universe is ordered. The times of the day and the seasons of the year reflect the rhythm of creation and the presence of the Creator. It is one reason we celebrate the Liturgy of the Hours and the liturgical year. Within the order of the universe we find an opportunity for grace.

The late Avery Cardinal Dulles tells a story of discovering the divine order in nature. Long before becoming a cardinal, he was a student at Harvard University. While a sophomore he had already shrugged off his family's Presbyterian faith. For him, religion belonged to the realm of superstition. He believed that human beings were produced by chance without any ordained end, and morality was merely a set of conventions woven together for convenience. The young Dulles favored "materialism," a philosophy that maintains that all of existence can be explained in material terms and there is no place for spirituality. All of creation is held together by matter and is subject to the laws of nature. This was his secular faith. Then one day, he went for a walk.

Dulles records this story in his autobiography, *A Testimonial to Grace*. He remembers, one day, studying in Harvard's Widener Library, poring over Augustine's *De Civitate Dei* for a course in medieval history. It was a gray day in February. On an impulse he closed the book and stepped outside for a breath of fresh air. He strayed toward the banks of the Charles River. While walking there he stopped to look at a young tree:

> On its frail, supple branches were young buds attending eagerly the spring which was at hand. While my eye rested on them the thought came to me suddenly, with all the strength and novelty of a revelation, that these little buds in their innocence and meekness followed a rule, a law of which I as yet knew nothing. How could it be, I asked, that this delicate tree sprang up and developed and that all the enormous complexity of its cellular operations combined together to make it grow erectly and bring forth leaves and

blossoms? The answer . . . [is] that its actions were ordered to an end by the only power capable of adapting means to ends—intelligence—and that the very fact that this intelligence worked toward an end implied purposiveness—in other words, a will. . . . The 'nature' which was responsible for these events was distinguished by the possession of intellect and will, and intellect plus will makes personality.

Dulles concludes, "Mind, then, not matter, was at the origin of all things." That night, he prayed for the first time in years. Like a schoolboy, he knelt by his bedside and prayed the Lord's Prayer, focusing on the words, "Thy will be done." He writes, "He was Our Father Who had made us; He had a will which was done in heaven."[3] And we can either accomplish this will or frustrate it. Dulles's spontaneous walk outdoors led him to contemplate a tree in winter and revealed the wondrous order of creation.

So why do you come to worship God? Is it to express your wonder, or to calm your fears? Do you believe that there is a rhythm to the world, or is it all merely random? Do we pray for grace or for luck?

Naming the Unknown God

Now let's turn to St. Paul. I think he can help us when he names the unknown god. In the Acts of the Apostles there is a scene where Paul preaches at a hill called the Areopagus. The hill had become a place for people to gather. It could be compared to a town square. Paul began by saying, "Athenians, I see how extremely religious you are in every way. For as I went through the city and looked carefully at the objects of your worship, I found among them an altar with the inscription, 'To an unknown god.' What therefore you worship as unknown, this I proclaim to you. The God who made the world and everything in it . . . so that they would search for God" (Acts 17:22-34).

Paul's speech formed a bridge between Christian monotheism and Greek polytheism. In his commentary on this passage, Luke Timothy Johnson points out that Paul does not criticize nor does he condemn Greek religion; rather, he recognizes it as a legitimate conversation partner in the approach to God. The longing for the

One whom all humans seek can provide the foundation for learning about the Lord of heaven and earth. Paul speaks to the incomplete longings of these "very religious" people and directs them to their proper object. He worked to understand their culture, to understand their longings, and direct them to the proper object of their desire, the One who is the Lord of all creation. It is a way of revealing the Holy Spirit that permeates the universe.

Paul understood his culture. He displays this understanding when he goes on to say, "Indeed [God] is not far from each one of us. For *'In him we live and move and have our being'*; as even some of your own poets have said" (vv. 27-28). The italicized line is found in Preface VI for the eucharistic prayer on Sundays in Ordinary Time. It is interesting to note that Paul may have borrowed this line from a Greek poet, Epimenides, who lived in the seventh century BCE. The poem is called "Cretica," and Epimenides dedicated it to Zeus, in defense of his immortality: "A grave have fashioned for thee, O holy and high One, the lying Cretans, who are all the time liars, evil beasts, idle bellies; but thou diest not, for to eternity thou livest and standest; for in thee we live, and move, and have our being."[4]

Like Paul, the preacher must be "bilingual," that is, the preacher must be able to speak in both the language of the tradition and the language of the culture. He must understand the Christian tradition, having knowledge of the Scripture and the teachings of the church. He must also have a facility to communicate with the culture in which he lives. The question that should be at the forefront of preaching is, how will those longing to see the face of God hear and receive the message?

Paul seems to catch glimpses of the Holy Spirit permeating creation and pointing to the Lord of heaven and earth. He widened the understanding of spirituality and allowed for dialogue between the Christians and the Greeks. In the twenty-first century, Christian preachers must still look for ways to widen the understanding of "spirituality" to include the longing of all people and direct them to the object of their prayer.

To widen our understanding of "spirituality" we might begin by asking what we mean by the word. This is one of those words we use regularly but it begs for an explanation. Consider this.

Roger Haight, in his book *Christian Spirituality for Seekers*, describes spirituality as "the fundamental organization of a person's life. It is the center of gravity that supplies coherence to the sum total of one's behavior."[5] All people have a spirituality in that their lives bear a certain consistency. One's spirituality both reflects and describes the story of one's life. In this sense we are all spiritual beings. Each of us must have a center of gravity to maintain consistency in our lives. The question we mean to ask here is, What is in your center? What guides you? What motivates you? What keeps you balanced through the twists and turns of your life? What is in your center? It is there that we find God. This is the basis of human spirituality.

Preaching "Catholic"

Now let us turn to Catholic preaching. What does it mean to preach "catholic"? Many of us learned the meaning of the word catholic back in parochial grade school. We were taught that catholic—with a small *c*—means "universal." And it still does. To which we could ask the question, What does it mean to say that the church is universal? And why is it that we call the church "catholic" rather than "universal"?

The phrase "the Catholic Church" may have originated in the early second century. The first time it is mentioned is in a letter from St. Ignatius of Antioch, the Epistle to the Smyrnaeans, written in the year 110. The Smyrnaeans formed one of the seven churches of Asia. Ignatius writes, "Wherever the bishop shall appear, there let the people be, even as where Jesus may be, there is the *katholikos* (Catholic) church." We also find the word *katholikos* in the Greek classics, for example, in Aristotle, as well as in the early Christian writers, such as Justin Martyr and Tertullian, among others. Their use of the word implies either "all-inclusive" or "universal."

The question still stands, why did the early Christians adopt the Greek word *katholikos* instead of the Latin word *universalis*? David O'Brien asks this question in an essay called "Conversations on Jesuit (and Catholic?) Higher Education." He explains that, technically, *katholikos* means "through the whole" or throughout the entirety. The Latin word *universalis* conveys a meaning of territory and jurisdiction, and it is the concern of a governing body. It is more of a legal term. But the Greek word suggests something different, something more like yeast. For example, remember when Jesus says, "[The kingdom of God] is like yeast that a woman took and mixed in with three measures of flour until all of it was leavened" (Luke 13:21). Jesus compares the kingdom of God to a growing reality that is limitless, one that is destined to be present everywhere and affecting everything. But note that yeast does not convert everything into itself. Yeast acts on the dough, but does not convert the dough into yeast. *Katholikos* implies "permeating" rather than "governing." The theologian Karl Rahner said that the church is really present almost everywhere. In each place it tries to build itself into the culture and incorporate the culture into itself. So, on the one hand, the church helps the world to rise to its goal as destined by God, like the yeast that gives rise to the bread. On the other hand, the church needs to collaborate with these cultures in order to penetrate all of God's creation. The church relies on the resources of a society's culture, especially the sciences and the arts, to permeate the world and find God's presence lurking in the natural world.

This notion of permeating the world is the basis for the "sacramental imagination." All creation manifests the presence of God. Since the world was created by God, and since human beings are made in the image and likeness of God, we learn something about God through our understanding of the world and of humanity. We gain a glimpse of God through creation. We know something of the Creator through the creation, just as we learn something about an artist through his or her work.

For example, recently I attended a performance of Mozart's opera *Don Giovanni* at the New York Metropolitan Opera House. Now, I am not a musician, nor do I consider myself a devotee of the opera—and I have never met Mozart. However, I could appreciate the genius of the man through his uplifting score, and I learned about his playful disposition in this comic opera. We learn something of the composer through the composition. Likewise, we learn something of the Creator through the creation.

It then stands to reason that the more we know about the creation, the more we will learn about the Creator. We rely on the secular to build up the sacred. This is to say that the secular study of science and the arts may help us to deepen our understanding of the world and of the human condition. And then we will learn how the Holy Spirit permeates creation.

To preach "catholic," that is, to preach in a Catholic manner, means to uncover the presence of God around us. It is a matter of "naming grace," as we discussed earlier. Think of the preaching of Jesus, especially with his parables, those short stories that were based on common events that presented a clear moral lesson. Jesus would show how grace was already at work within and around his gathering, and how they needed to let it grow, like yeast rising within the dough.

Grace builds on nature. Grace is working within us like the yeast within the rising loaf of bread. From this we know something about how God works. The preacher opens up the Scripture by showing how Jesus, the Son of God, deals with us.

CHAPTER FOUR

Jesus Christ, the Story of God

In the beginning was the Word, and the Word was with
God, and the Word was God.

—John 1:1

The story of Jesus Christ is the "greatest story ever told." The
prologue of the Gospel of John gives us the introduction to that
story. John writes, "In the beginning was the Word, and the Word
was with God, and the Word was God. He was in the beginning
with God. All things came into being through him, and without
him not one thing came into being. What has come into being in
him was life, and the life was the light of all people" (John 1:1-4).
Jesus Christ, the second person of the Blessed Trinity, is the Word
of God. Christ is the Word that God speaks to the world. German
theologian Hans Urs von Balthasar described the Trinity as an act
of speech. Every act of speech consists of a speaker, a word, and
the breath that animates the voice and enables the word to be
spoken. Without breath we cannot speak; our words will not be
heard. Within the Trinity the Father is the speaker, the Son is the
word, and the Holy Spirit is the breath.

God's word calls all of creation into being. We might think of
the word of God as the story of the Father, the one who speaks.
Jesus Christ is God's story. The Father reveals himself through the
Son. God wishes to be revealed so that all human beings may come
to know him as their source and destiny. Jesus Christ is the way
in which we know the Father. As he said, "No one knows the

Father except the Son and anyone to whom the Son chooses to reveal him" (Matt 11:27). He also said, "Whoever has seen me has seen the Father" (John 14:9). Jesus shows us the Father. His stories, often in the form of parables, describe the kingdom of heaven and the mercy of God. We hear how the kingdom of heaven is like a banquet table prepared by a generous lord. Or it is like a mustard tree with sprawling branches where the birds come to build their nests. God's mercy is like a shepherd searching for one lost sheep, or a woman scouring the house for one lost coin, or a father awaiting the return of his wayward son. Jesus Christ tells stories about his Father and the realm of heaven. And more than this, Jesus Christ himself is the story of God. The way Jesus lived, acted, and spoke, on earth, revealed "Emmanuel," God with us; Jesus named grace.

Stories are the way we reveal ourselves to one another. It is the way we come to know each other. We do not come to know our friends by collecting data on them. The numbers that identify us do not matter all that much on a personal level: our date of birth, height and weight, social security number—this is the concern for a security agency. But friends and neighbors gather stories and come to know one another this way.

Jesus Christ is the story of God. He is the way we come to know the Father. For this reason it is important that the preacher tell the story of Jesus for the faithful who have come to worship because they long to see the Lord. The members of the congregation are like the people we hear about in the Gospel of John, the ones who approached the disciple Philip, and said to him, "Sir, we wish to see Jesus" (John 12:21). The preacher, like Philip, provides an opportunity for the faithful to encounter God. And they will encounter God through hearing the story of Jesus Christ once again. Perhaps we can find a comparison between these ancient Greeks and our modern congregation. They come to "see" Jesus, but in a way that transcends physical sight. Throughout John's gospel we find invitations to see the Lord, as when two disciples of John the Baptist pursue Jesus and ask him, "Rabbi, . . . where are you staying?" Jesus replies, "Come and see" (1:38-39). For John the evangelist, this use of "see" calls for an in-depth look at Jesus that will lead a follower to either accept or reject him. We might translate the plea of the Greeks to Philip as, "Sir, we would like to understand Jesus." Consider too that these Greeks do not stroll casually to see Jesus. They come amidst a maelstrom of political activity. At this point there is growing interest in Jesus. Shortly before this episode, a crowd of people stood in amazement as they watched Lazarus, still wrapped like a mummy, walk out of his tomb. They wondered about Jesus and his ability to raise the dead. In the following scene, Martha and Mary host a dinner party, and their brother Lazarus is at table. Sometime during the meal, Mary knelt by Jesus' feet, anointing them with an expensive ointment and drying them with her long hair. Mary's gesture becomes a foreshadowing of Jesus' death, a symbolic embalming of Jesus, following the custom of the day, to anoint a body before burial.

All this happened near the city of Jerusalem and around the time of the Passover. This season was charged with both spiritual and political meaning. The Israelites looked back in their history, commemorating their freedom from bondage, led by Moses to the Promised Land. They looked forward as well, to the day when a new liberator would free them from Roman rule. Many expected Jesus of Nazareth to be the long-awaited Messiah. So one day they lined the road leading to Jerusalem, waving palm branches at him as he rode a donkey into the city. Jesus appeared to be a prince, but clearly a prince of peace. The curiosity and enthusiasm that swelled around Jesus stirred panic among the chief priests and Pharisees. They said, "You see, you can do nothing. Look, the world has gone after him!" (John 12:19). So they drew up an order for his arrest.

In the midst of all this spiritual fervor and political excitement, these Greeks ask to see Jesus. Are they not like many seekers today, searching for spirituality, and hoping to recognize their own story in Jesus Christ? On any given Sunday the preacher stands with Philip and greets the faithful who, in their own way, echo the Greeks, saying, "Sir, we wish to see Jesus." Then the preacher turns to the Lord and prays, "This is the people that longs to see your face."

The foundation of this story is the paschal mystery, the belief that Jesus Christ is the incarnate Word of God, and through his humiliating death and glorious resurrection, he has become the Savior of the world. This story may be told in many ways. The paschal mystery is like a multifaceted diamond with each piece giving a glimpse of the whole. The Sundays of the year, as well as the holy days and feasts, along with the daily celebration of the Eucharist, show us these facets of our faith. They are variations on a theme, all pointing to the Son of God and uncovering the paschal mystery. The paschal mystery is the theme of our worship.

Whose Story Is It?

Speaking of a "theme," we sometimes hear the planners of a liturgy talk about the "theme for today's liturgy." This seems to suggest that the planners intend to impose a point of focus on the celebration of the liturgy. We need to be clear: There is but one "theme" for the Liturgy of the Eucharist, and that is the paschal mystery. This is the one and only "theme." This is what we celebrate whenever we gather for Eucharist. The words of the liturgy ring out to us, "Behold the Lamb of God." These words call our attention to the sacrificial Lamb who was slain for the sake of our salvation. "Behold," for God stands among us, here and now. In a sense, our liturgy poses the question, Where may we find the Lord today?

We should beware of losing focus and making the liturgy a story of ourselves. To talk of liturgical themes other than the paschal mystery may shift the focus from God to the congregation. Take, for example, Mother's Day. We could ask, should we celebrate Mother's Day during Mass? Now, surely it is good that society dedicates a day to celebrate our mothers. It should be apparent that mothers hold a most important place in society, not to mention in our personal lives. We should take time to celebrate our mothers as a sign of respect and appreciation. And we can also ask, in the context of this discussion, what will this celebration sound like within the liturgy? Will we hear preaching that extolls the virtues of motherhood with stories of the preacher's mother and grandmother? And will Jesus Christ be left in the sacristy as we shift our focus to the mothers of the parish? Or can this day become an occasion when we understand the paschal mystery in a new way? Perhaps we can learn something new about the love of God through the love of a good mother. Indeed, if we have experienced a mother's love, then we know something about the love of God. As Jesus said, using the metaphor of a mother,

"Jerusalem . . . How often have I desired to gather your children together as a hen gathers her brood under her wings" (Matt 23:37). The point is that we keep the focus on Jesus Christ and show how a mother's love shines a light on the paschal mystery.

I can remember well the words of a mother as she delivered the eulogy for her teenaged son. He had been killed in a diving accident. It was late at night, at the home of a friend, when he leaped from a diving board into a pool, not realizing that the water was quite shallow. At the memorial service, his mother spoke of how she went to the hospital to identify the body of her son. In viewing the mangled corpse she said, "This is my body." Those words have taken on new meaning for me when I celebrate the Eucharist. A mother's love may open up the story of Jesus Christ who is the story of God. Likewise, the paschal mystery may give new meaning to motherhood. Mother's Day is about more than flowers and chocolates. When we celebrate Mother's Day within the Eucharist, we may understand God's love and mercy in a new way. What is important here is that we keep focused on Jesus Christ and his story. Preaching is sacramental and, like all the sacraments, it needs to point to God. "Keep your eyes on the prize," as the folk song says, or else we will lose focus and we may end up worshiping ourselves.

Knowing Our Story as Part of *the* Story

By hearing the story of Jesus Christ again, we will come to know our own story in a fuller way. The homily helps the faithful to interpret their lives. This is one more purpose of preaching, enabling the disciples of today to understand their lives in relation to Jesus Christ. The way in which we understand our lives—our meaning and reason for being—is learned through interpretation. Human understanding is a process by which we relate a new experience to what we already know through previous study or past experience. Our understanding of mathematical formulas builds upon our prior knowledge of the principles of arithmetic. Our understanding of other people—our classmates and colleagues and those we encounter on a daily basis—derives from our interactions and relations with the many people who fill our lives. We interpret our lives through categories of understanding.

For example, I have had the great opportunity to teach abroad. I have spent time in classrooms in Nairobi, Kenya, and in Katmandu, Nepal. While my time there was enjoyable and memorable, I did experience some culture shock. I remember well the first day of each course, filled with a teacher's anxiety of meeting a new class and, in this case, how "foreign," that is, how different, it all looked to me. On the first day of a class most teachers I know are nervous; much of that has to do with meeting a new "audience" for the first time. We may be familiar with the material but not so familiar with the class sitting before us. Teaching within a foreign culture exaggerated this anxiety. However, in each case I found that once I became engaged with the students—once the first question was asked—I recognized that I was on familiar ground and could relate comfortably to the students. They were not so strange after all.

Mary Catherine Hilkert explains that we interpret our lives through a framework of understanding. As she says, "Human life is always interpreted in the context of the multiple traditions within which one stands, including personal history, family stories, ethnic roots, and culture. New experiences may call for modification, change, or even rejection of previous horizons, but initially all human experience occurs within some framework of meaning that has been handed on. Children are born into systems of language and cultural symbols; they do not create them."[1] Perhaps Hilkert's framework of understanding is one more example of Qoheleth's oracle: "There is nothing new under the sun."

We Christians find meaning in our lives by understanding the life of Jesus Christ. The Christian story provides a framework of understanding. Let's return to the gospel story of the two disciples on the road to Emmaus. As the two men walked away from Jerusalem, they were weighed down with confusion and worry. The sadness of Jesus' death and the rumor of his resurrection challenged their faith. What were these two faithful followers of Jesus to make of all of this? Were they wrong to believe that Jesus was the Messiah? Along the way they met the stranger who would open the Scripture for them, and they would recognize him in the breaking of the bread. They recognized that Jesus was the one of whom the prophets spoke; he was the fulfillment of the covenantal prophecy. And immediately they went out to share the good news with the other disciples. Jesus, the living Word of God, enabled the two disciples to interpret their experience. Through this interpretation, the story of Jesus Christ was no longer just "a story," but it became their story, the narrative that filled their lives with meaning.

In speaking about this passage in their book *Preaching the Mystery of Faith*, the US bishops comment, "The sacred writings of the Old Testament, which these disciples knew well, now took on a new resonance as they were placed in relation to Jesus and his life-giving Death and Resurrection."[2] The bishops compare the congregation of today with the two disciples on their way to Emmaus, and worry that the current congregation may also be headed in the wrong direction. When Jesus opened the Scriptures for the pair of disciples he offered a model for a homily. We could say that he followed Augustine's threefold purpose of preaching. First, Jesus taught them something new; then he delighted them, that is to say, they were inspired by him; and then they were moved to action. He taught them so that their understanding of the Scripture was deepened. He delighted them, for, in the words of the bishops, he touched them at "the deepest levels of the human heart and address[ed] the real questions of human experience."[3] He moved them so that they ran out to inform the other followers of Jesus and went about spreading the good news. Jesus' preaching enabled those who would listen to him to interpret their experience in such a way that they would find themselves within the story of Jesus Christ.

In his book *Christian Eloquence: Contemporary Doctrinal Preaching*, Colt Anderson says, "The world is like a book that has to be interpreted."[4] However, he points out a problem, namely, that there is a great challenge to interpreting this "book." The problem is caused by sin, which renders the book unintelligible to us. Sin distorts our understanding of reality. The scriptural story teaches us how to dig deeper into reality and to find the sacramental meaning of the world. Christian faith provides a point of contact joining the readers with the Scripture and the worlds around them.

Each of us has a story that integrates all the aspects of our lives. The individual story helps each of us to understand how we relate to the world around us. Where and when we were born, and to whom, holds a great influence upon us. (When people ask me why I am a Catholic, I answer that, first of all, it has something to do with these three factors. If you were like me and born in the mid-1950s, in the borough of Brooklyn of New York City, to an Italian-American family, there is a good chance that you would have been baptized and raised in the Catholic Church. Of course, as we mature, we eventually have to make the choice for ourselves, a personal choice to follow Christ in the church.)

Political and cultural movements matter as well, along with our socioeconomic class and level of education. And we should not forget friendships and romantic relationships, some that are lasting, others fleeting. These and other qualities contribute to our personal story. Again, this story helps us to understand who we are in the midst of the world, and it is the way we present ourselves to others.

But as human beings, along with knowing who we are, it is essential to know why we are here. This is to say that we inquire seriously into the meaning of our lives. To answer this question of meaning we need to relate our own story to a grand story, an overarching narrative that includes all stories. Within this grand narrative we recognize the intersection of individual stories, the points where our lives connect with others. For example, I once heard the Dalai Lama say to an audience how we are all quite similar in that each of us seeks happiness and avoids sadness; all of us share these traits. Mahatma Gandhi said that "suffering is the badge of the human race," meaning that all people share the experience of suffering. While we do not suffer in the same way, we all do suffer, so that we may relate to the suffering of others. And we may wonder if Jesus appealed to a universal trait of compassion when he saved the life of the woman caught in adultery by saying to the bloodthirsty crowd, "Let anyone among you who is without sin be the first to throw a stone at her" (John 8:7). In this dramatic moment, did the crowd recognize their own sinfulness, reducing their ability to stand in judgment of another person? The grand narrative is the story through which we understand our lives in relation to a greater story. Through this grand narrative our individual stories come to life in a new way, much like the disciples at Emmaus hearing the Scripture retold to them. We are always interpreting our experiences, wondering what meaning they hold for us. Joyful events, such as the birth of a baby or a wedding, bring new meaning to people, extending their web of relationships. Those who join in the celebration come to understand themselves in a new way. In tragic times, such as the sudden death of a loved one from illness or a suicide, the family and friends may be left to search for meaning in the face of seeming absurdity.

Knowing our own stories in relation to the grand narrative may give us the courage to carry on in a time of crisis. Recall how the African-American slaves suffered such cruel degradation. They were considered by many to be merely human chattel, a commodity to be traded on the market. These slaves recognized their plight in relation to the story of the ancient Hebrews who were enslaved in Egypt. The story of the Hebrews' captivity and exodus empowered the American slaves to recognize their forced servitude to be immoral. They knew that God did not intend for them to suffer this way, for they, too, were made in the image and likeness of the Creator. So when the white preachers attempted to explain that it was God's will for them to be slaves, the black congregation listened with a filtering ear, ignoring the corruption of the Scripture. And they waited for the day when their liberator, Jesus Christ, would lead them to the Promised Land. Knowing our personal stories in relation to the grand narrative helps us to find the meaning of our lives, enabling us to celebrate the joyful moments, and emboldening us to endure the suffering that comes to us all. Jesus Christ reveals the story of God's freedom.

Finally, stories are part of our Judeo-Christian heritage. Through stories we pass on our religious tradition. The preacher, then, is the storyteller for the community. Some may be familiar with this Chasidic tale, as told by Elie Wiesel:

> When the great Rabbi Israel Bal Shem-Tov saw misfortune threatening the Jews it was his custom to go into a certain part of the forest to meditate. There he would light a fire, say a special prayer, and the miracle would be accomplished and the misfortune averted.
>
> Later, when his disciple, the celebrated Magid of Mezritch, had occasion, for the same reason, to intercede with heaven, he would go to the same place in the forest and say: "Master of the Universe, listen! I do not know how to light the fire, but I am still able to say the prayer." And again the miracle would be accomplished.

Still later, Rabbi Moshe-Leib of Sasov, in order to save his people once more, would go into the forest and say: "I do not know how to light the fire, I do not know the prayer, but I know the place and this must be sufficient." It was sufficient and the miracle was accomplished. Then it fell to Rabbi Israel of Rizhyn to overcome misfortune. Sitting in his armchair, his head in his hands, he spoke to God: "I am unable to light the fire and I do not know the prayer; I cannot even find the place in the forest. All I can do is to tell the story, and this must be sufficient." And it was sufficient. God created [humankind] because He loves stories.[5]

The preacher helps the faithful to tell their stories to God.

PART II

"Sit Down *Before* You Preach!"
A Method of Preparation

Some time ago I attended an ordination of Jesuit deacons at St. Paul's Church located in Harvard Square, Cambridge, Massachusetts. An auxiliary bishop of Boston, the Very Rev. John Banks, would ordain twelve Jesuits that morning. On a crisp fall day, the church was packed with family and friends of the *ordinandi*. A large company of concelebrants assisted the bishop. A cheerful air of celebration filled the church.

Immediately following the proclamation of the gospel, the bishop delivered his homily. He began by saying, "The problem with most preachers is that they don't know when to sit down." The congregation paused and then roared with laughter. With that one line the bishop managed to turn a rather formal ceremony into a revival meeting. You could hear shouts of "Amen" and "Yes." Someone shouted, "Finally someone has heard us." The bishop let the laughter continue. And when the noise subsided he added, "Oh, I mean, sit down *before* they preach." The church grew still. He went on, "I mean to sit down to pray and prepare." The message was clear. He was not pandering to the crowd, nor was he telling a joke to get them warmed up. He was about to offer an important instruction for preachers and went on to speak about the importance of preparation in preaching.

Preachers need to take time to prepare a homily. Since my ordination in 1986 I have come to appreciate that preaching is difficult. Like the Buddha's first truth, "Life is difficult," I have adopted the mantra, "Preaching is difficult."

Preaching takes time, and it is hard work. One seminary dean told me that there was a need to develop a culture of preparation. He noted that for many preachers, their preparation for the Sunday sermon took place in the shower that morning, stringing together a few thoughts before dashing off to church. He asked me, "Is this the best we can do? Is this all we can offer the people of God?"

The dean's advice is well taken. We need to develop a culture of preparation, taking the time to prepare to preach. It seems that when we hear complaints about preaching they are not due to the preacher's lack of brilliance or eloquence, but more from a lack of diligence. Preachers need to take the time to pray over the meaning of the Scripture and consider the needs of the congregation. They need to take time to research the historical background and theological themes of the Scripture. They need to take time to think through and rehearse the homily, asking if the message is clear and how the congregation will hear it. They need to sit down before they preach.

Father Walter Burghardt, SJ, one of the renowned Catholic preachers in the United States, recommended a preparation time of one hour for every minute in the pulpit. So if he planned to preach for ten minutes he would spend ten hours in preparation. Clearly Fr. Burghardt did not mean that he sat at his desk for ten hours straight, crafting the homily. Rather, the preparation period is cumulative. It includes the time we spend in reading and praying with the Scripture, the time we spend in studying the commentaries and other sources, the time given to talking with others, the time spent in drafting the homily and shaping it for the congregation whom we will meet on Sunday. Add this all together and there is a good chance that we will meet Burghardt's formula of one hour per minute. The preparation time is spread throughout the week, and it helps to begin early.

Also, we do not have to work alone. I have found it beneficial to begin the work with other preachers. For example, on Monday evening, after dinner, a few members of my Jesuit community meet to read the Scriptures for the following Sunday. The meeting lasts about forty-five minutes. We read the Scripture aloud, one person taking the gospel, another the Old Testament reading, then the psalm, and then the New Testament. After some quiet time we talk about what comes to mind, such as a word or phrase we heard in a new way, a striking image, or a challenging command. All the while we wonder how our particular congregations will hear this passage. For example, one will preach to a university congregation. Another to an urban Latino parish. One other takes a convent call each Sunday morning. We end with a discussion around the question, "So what's the good news?" This weekly meeting requires no preparation except to bring a copy of the Scripture for next Sunday. It is an opportunity to "prime the pump," that is, to begin the preaching process by reading the Scriptures early and begin culling ideas for a homily, with the added benefit of hearing from others. This process wards off the Saturday night scavenger hunt. I have suffered through this—the desperate search for something to say the next day. Like the college freshman cramming to write a term paper from scratch the night before it is due, very little creativity occurs here and the task is pure drudgery.

Another process I found helpful is one practiced at Santa Clara University. During a sabbatical year there I took a regular turn at presiding and preaching with the campus ministry liturgies for Sunday. The students would pack the church on Sunday evening. The participation was strong, no doubt due to the great preparation in word and song. Two weeks before the scheduled liturgy the ministers meet to "break open the word." The chaplain, the liturgical coordinator, the cantor and the music director, the student readers, and the presider/preacher gather faithfully. They meet solely to listen to the word of God. For the preacher it is very helpful to hear the students comment on the passages that will be proclaimed that Sunday. It is a way to learn how this congregation will hear the Scripture and what resonates with them, for example, the images that spur their imagination or the phrases that confuse them, crying out for explanation. The group opens a window to the culture of college life. They provide the preacher a connection with the audience and a direction to follow. And, with two weeks to prepare, there is time to develop these ideas.

Whether we begin on Monday night or Saturday afternoon, we may end up putting in the same number of hours of preparation, but most likely the product will not be the same. This is something

I learned from my father, watching him make the sauce for our family's Sunday dinner. My father worked as an accountant Monday through Friday, but on weekends he became the family chef. When he planned to make lasagna for Sunday afternoon he would start the sauce on Friday night. After dinner, when the dishes were done and the table cleaned, he would place a large pot on the stove, over a low flame. On the kitchen counter the ingredients for the sauce were displayed. He poured into the pot a large can of tomato sauce and scooped in a small glob of tomato paste. In another pan sausage meat sizzled. He chopped some carrots, celery, and garlic, and slid them into the mix. Then he added olive oil, a pinch of sugar, flakes of red pepper, and a shot or two of red wine. When the sausage meat browned he poured it into the pot. He stirred the sauce, tasting it, and then let it simmer awhile. Later he turned off the flame and the pot of sauce sat on the back burner all through Saturday and Sunday morning. On Sunday afternoon he warmed the sauce and then poured it throughout the lasagna. Sitting down to dinner we all tasted a delicious meal of pasta and sauce.

I imagine that he could have made the sauce early Sunday afternoon, but it could never be the same. If you know sauce, you know it couldn't be. When you let the sauce rest for a day and a half you give all the ingredients a chance to blend—or to "marry," as the French say—producing a rich, delicious flavor. The sauce was "working" even while my father was away from the kitchen. Of course, if one has no taste for homemade sauce, a jar from the local supermarket will serve the purpose, but the taste will be bland. The point is that the preparation for the sauce, whether my father begins on Friday evening or Sunday afternoon, requires the same amount of work. It is when he begins that makes all the difference.

When we prepare to preach early in the week we place the ideas, images, and questions on the back burner of the brain. Then during the week ideas may begin to merge. A book or article we read, a movie we see or a song we hear, a conversation with a friend . . . any one of these may provide an insight. If we do not prepare early there will be no connection between an experience and the Scripture for Sunday. To be sure, this is not a formula for preparing to preach but more of a method. There is no guarantee that a homily will emerge from this process, but without it, we will probably preach a bland homily. Such a method of preparation allows for creativity and expression, much more than we can get from the scavenger hunt on Saturday night.

As the seminary dean said, we need to develop a culture of preparation. As part of this culture every preacher should have a method, that is, a regular process of preparation. The US bishops explain the need for a "homiletic method" in their document *Fulfilled in Your Hearing*:

> Artists who are conscious of their method are in a much more advantageous position than those who are not. They are able to channel and direct their work more easily, can work more efficiently within time constraints, and can adapt their method to changed circumstances and demands. They know what they are doing and how they go about doing it, and they can pass this information on to others who might like to learn from them.[1]

The bishops go on to say that the most important feature of a method is that it must be orderly and regular. The total amount of time spent in preparation is not as important as observing a regular pattern of activity spread out over a certain period of time.

I will propose one method here, which I refer to as the four Rs: reflect, research, write, and rehearse. These four stages should be spread throughout the week. For a suggested schedule I recommend beginning with the reflection on Monday by reading and praying over the Scripture for the following Sunday. On Wednesday, turn to the commentaries and other sources for research. On Friday, write up a draft of the homily, subject to revision. Finally on Saturday, rehearse the presentation, listening to how it will sound. Now let's discuss each of these stages.

CHAPTER FIVE

Reflect: First We Listen

The Word of God precedes us; certainly we interpret, but
first we listen.

—Fred Craddock, paraphrasing Karl Barth

We begin the process of preparing to preach by reading and reflecting upon the Scripture. Before asking what we can say *about*
the Scripture, we should ask, what does the Scripture say to us?
This is God's word that comes intruding upon our world, inter-
rupting business as usual, and interpreting our lives. So, before
consulting the commentaries and other resources for research, we
need to take time to pray and to allow the word of God to speak
to us, heeding the words of the psalm, "Be still, and know that I
am God!" (Ps 46:10).

In "listening" to the Scripture passages it will help to "hear"
them in conversation with one another. The Lectionary is designed
for such a conversation. In the arrangement of the readings for
Sunday, the gospel passage was chosen first. The gospel stands at
the center. Then the Old Testament passage is chosen, in light of
the gospel. The responsorial psalm responds to the Old Testament
reading. Father John Endres, SJ, a Scripture scholar and a specialist
in the Psalms, once mentioned to me that when he is preparing
to preach, he will ask, "Who in the Old Testament reading is speaking the psalm?" The responsorial psalm gives voice to the people's
hope that the message of the Old Testament will be fulfilled. The
New Testament reading follows a separate path, one of *lectio*

continua, or a "continuous reading." This second reading was added in response to a directive stated in *Sacrosanctum Concilium* to provide a richer fare of Scripture within the liturgy. Throughout the liturgical cycles we will hear a semi-continuous reading from the epistles. Note that the second reading is not connected explicitly to the gospel and the Old Testament readings. Nevertheless, the preacher, reading all four passages together in preparation of the homily, may find that new meaning is uncovered.

Here are two suggestions for prayer while preparing to preach. One is the ancient practice of *lectio divina* (divine reading), which is a slow, reflective reading of the text. We read the Scripture like we are reading a letter from a friend, a message deepening our friendship. Read slowly, savoring the words. We are not reading for comprehension, as a student would in preparing for class. With *lectio divina* the reading becomes personal. We realize that this is God's word for us. We pay attention to which words and images stand out in the reading. Has the reading conjured up any emotions? Do we feel happy, sad, confirmed, confused, etc.? Is there some new discovery in this reading, something we have not noticed in the many times we have read and heard the story? Does the reading raise a question for reflection or study?

For example, in preparing to preach for the vigil Mass of the birth of John the Baptist, a question loomed at me from the gospel: Why was Zechariah punished for questioning the angel Gabriel? Gabriel announced to Zechariah, an elderly priest of the temple, that his wife, Elizabeth, would bear a son. (Luke 5:1-23—I have included several more verses than we find in the Lectionary reading for the day.) Remember that Elizabeth was thought to be barren. Moreover, their son would play a significant role in the divine plan for salvation. Zechariah was confused by the announcement and asked for a sign. But the only sign he received was to be rendered mute. He did not speak again until after the birth of his son, the one he named "John." In reading this well-known passage again, and preparing to preach for the vigil Mass, I needed to ask, "Why was Zechariah punished?" We will continue with this question presently, but for now, we may find that, through the slow and deliberate process of *lectio divina*, new questions and insights may arise from an old and familiar story.

Another method for praying with Scripture comes from the *Spiritual Exercises* of St. Ignatius of Loyola, and is called "contemplation of place." To enter into this form of prayer Ignatius recommends that you place yourself in the biblical scene. You may imagine yourself as one of the characters in the story. Begin by reading the passage. Then imagine you are in the location by engaging all your senses with the details of the story. What do you see, hear, feel, taste, or smell?

To illustrate this method of prayer, let us return to the annunciation to Zechariah. Note that this is the opening scene in the Gospel of Luke. The gospel begins with an eloquent prologue in which Luke explains the purpose for his writing this book (Luke 1:1-4). Following the prologue we can imagine the story being staged. The curtain is drawn and we see the elderly Zechariah standing in the temple, preparing to burn the incense, which was one of his priestly duties. Off to the side, on a separate stage, we glance at Elizabeth at home, going through her daily chores. Outside the temple stands a crowd of people, praying aloud. Then the angel Gabriel appears. (What would the angel look like? Is it a man with wings, dressed in white? Or is the angel simply a beam of light?)

First we try to see the stage with its set and characters in place. What do they look like? What are they wearing? Then we may feel some physical sensations: Is it hot or cold, dry or damp? Can we smell the incense burning in the temple? Do we taste anything? Finally, listen to the conversation between the angel and the priest. Note that at first, Zechariah is frightened by the appearance of Gabriel. The angel tries to convey a joyful message, but Zechariah cannot receive it joyfully. Either he is incredulous or simply stubborn. We hear Gabriel change his tone of voice, from jubilant to stern as he tells Zechariah, "You will be silent." Then we watch Zechariah leave the temple dumbstruck while the crowd watches and wonders at what took place inside. The next scene brings good news. Elizabeth indeed has conceived. But we may wonder about the period in between, when Zechariah returned home, mute, and he and his wife were left to ponder the meaning of Gabriel's good news.

Let us try to focus more closely on the scene. For this, I find Brendan Byrne's commentary *The Hospitality of God: A Reading of*

Luke's Gospel to be a good resource. First we see the great temple of Jerusalem, the traditional place of reconciliation between God and the Jewish people. Luke begins and ends the gospel here in the temple. Then Luke describes Zechariah and Elizabeth as two devout Jews, who are "righteous before God, living blamelessly according to all the commandments and regulations of the Lord" (1:6). However, they both suffered the shame of being childless; they were incapable of continuing the family line. The scene is fraught with tension. Here are two righteous and pious people who lack the blessing of a child. Then Gabriel bursts into the scene, striking fear into Zechariah. Note that whenever an angel appears in these early chapters of Luke's gospel, he strikes fear into those he visits. We hear this first with Zechariah in the temple, then with Mary in Nazareth, and then with the shepherds in Bethlehem. The divine intrusion is clearly awesome and each time the angel needs to assure those he visits by saying, "Do not be afraid."

As a devout Jew Zechariah stands in a somewhat familiar position, an echo of the past. This is to say that he would have remembered the great leaders of Israel and how their births were announced by a messenger, or angel, from God. For example, the story of the birth of Samson foreshadows the birth of John the Baptist (Judg 13:2-7). Zechariah would have remembered, as well, the stories of a barren woman being promised a child and how that promise was fulfilled, as in the stories of Hannah, the mother of Samuel (1 Sam 1:1-28), and Sara, the wife of Abraham and mother of Isaac (Gen 16:1). According to Byrne, "The motif of childlessness implies a blockage on the human side that only God's power can overcome."[1] If Israel is to experience new life and leadership, it will come about solely through the direct action of God. However, Zechariah appears to resist God's action. Perhaps his fear gets the best of him. Aware of his wife's advanced age and her condition, he asks for a sign. He articulates the "blockage on the human side." It would seem to be a reasonable request; nevertheless, he receives a harsh response. He is struck dumb, and unable to speak until the promise is fulfilled.

As an aside, could this case be similar to the "confession of Peter"? Recall the story found in the Gospel of Matthew when Jesus takes the disciples aside and predicts his passion. He told them of how he would suffer, how he would be rejected by the elders and then killed, and on the third day rise again (Matt 16:21-23). After hearing this, Peter boldly spoke up, challenging Jesus and promising, "This must never happen to you." But Jesus rebuked him sternly, "Get behind me, Satan! You are a stumbling block to me." We can imagine Peter's good intention, an expression of his devotion to Jesus. So Jesus' rebuke may sound harsh, like the angel Gabriel responding to Zechariah. But here again, we find an example of the "blockage on the human side," a hindrance to furthering the kingdom of God. Sometimes, even with the best of intentions, Jesus' followers may be blocking the good news of salvation.

For Zechariah, his punishment may serve as a warning. Something new is happening that requires extraordinary faith, the kind of faith that Mary displays at her own annunciation. The only sign Zechariah receives is to be rendered mute. It is a sign of his inadequate response to the angel. Sometimes we must remain mute before mystery.

Through the use of the contemplation of place we insert ourselves into the Bible story. In this case, we identified with one of the characters, Zechariah, trying to see and hear as he would. This exercise may help us to experience the passage in a new way and reveal a deeper understanding. Through praying with the Scripture, either by *lectio divina* or a "contemplation of place," we may uncover fresh insights from old stories. Then we have something to take with us for research.

But before opening the commentaries, preachers should ask another question: Where do they stand in relation to the congregation? How does the preacher understand his role amidst the people of God? We might diagram an act of public speaking as a triangle. The ancient philosopher Aristotle describes such a diagram in his classic work *Rhetoric*. He explains that there are three points within any public speech: the audience, the speaker, and the message. We just discussed the relationship of the preacher with the Scripture, emphasizing that the word of God must speak to the preacher before the preacher can speak about the word of God. Now we want to ask, where does the preacher stand in relation to those who will hear the word of God? For Aristotle and the orators of ancient Greece and Rome, the first rule of public speaking was "know your audience": the speaker must consider who is in the audience and imagine how they will hear the message.

Pope Francis expressed this relationship well in his address to the priests of the world at the Chrism Mass on Holy Thursday, 2013: "The priest who seldom goes out of himself . . . misses out on the best of our people, on what can stir the depths of his priestly heart. . . . This is precisely the reason for the dissatisfaction of some, who end up . . . sad priests—in some sense becoming collectors of antiquities or novelties, instead of being shepherds living with 'the odour of the sheep.' This I ask you: be shepherds, with the 'odour of the sheep.' "[2]

Everyone who studies Scripture learns how to exegete a passage. Appreciating the literary and historical context of a pericope opens the text for fresh understanding. In a similar way we could say that the preacher needs to exegete the congregation. In other words, the preacher needs to know who is sitting in the congregation. There is no such thing as a "typical" congregation. Each one carries its own characteristics. Richard Lischer, in his book *Theories of Preaching*, writes of a long list of opposites taken from Gregory the Great.[3] Writing in his *Pastoral Rule* in the sixth century, Gregory drew up a list of thirty-six "pairs of opposites" whom he could find in a congregation. He listed them as men and women, young and old, rich and poor, the joyful and the sad, the wise of this world and the dull, the slothful and the hasty, the humble and the haughty, the gluttonous and the abstinent, those who are bound by wedlock and those who are free from the ties of wedlock, those who have had experience of carnal intercourse and those who are ignorant of it. To this lengthy list we might add: those who came to church today, willingly, and those who had to be dragged inside. Gregory intended to address the problem of a mixed audience, which is created by the intellectual, social, and economic diversity that we find at most liturgical gatherings. To simplify Gregory's long list we may want to focus on the congregation and consider their range of age, the socioeconomic status, the level of education, ethnicity, and political affiliation. Also, it may help to know what these people do for recreation, their choice of reading (books, newspapers, magazines, digital or print), music (popular, classical, jazz, hip-hop), movies or theater, restaurants (fast food or French, Italian, Chinese, Mexican), sports (football or volleyball or golf), and entertainment in general. We want to know the congregation well enough in order to communicate clearly to them and to make the message of the gospel accessible. In the words of Augustine, citing again his book *On Christian Doctrine*, "Since there is some comparison between eating and learning, it may be noted that on account of the fastidiousness of many, even the food without which life is impossible, must be seasoned" (4.11.26). Exegeting the congregation allows the preacher to apply the right seasoning to the homily. Let's return to the question of where the preacher stands in relation to the congregation.

In preaching classes and workshops I will ask the students how they would describe God to a child. Specifically, I ask what adjectives and nouns they would use. For instance, do you think of God as a mother or father, a brother or sister, a good friend? You may imagine God as a doctor, a judge, or a boss. Chances are, our perception of God will influence our preaching. I can talk all day long, quoting St. John, that "God is love" (1 John 4:16), but if I really imagine God to be a tyrannical boss, ordering me to construct his kingdom on earth; or if I see God as a stern judge, meting out justice and fairness; then that is what people will hear, that God is a boss or a judge. My image of God must be clear to me if I am to convey it to the people before me.

Think of the African-American slaves and what they heard from the white preachers. These African-Americans were encouraged to be obedient slaves and that God would reward them in the next world. ("There will be pie in the sky in the great bye and bye!") But the slaves listened with a filtering ear. They knew that the God who freed the Israelites from bondage in Egypt and called them his chosen people did not want his own to suffer. This treatment degraded their humanity and denied the presence of God in the world. We should remember the words of St. Irenaeus who claimed that the glory of God is the person, fully human and fully alive. Anything that degrades human dignity is not of God. Here is one more image of God: the Almighty One who upholds human dignity. Who is God for you?

Another question I will ask the class is to remember a good homily or sermon they have heard. It could be either recent (within the past month), or remote (remembered from a long time ago). I then ask them to write a paragraph explaining why they considered this homily to be good. The answers compiled over the years are fairly consistent. Some comment that the preacher was well prepared because he understood the Scripture readings and knew how to present the message to the congregation. Others note the preacher's sincerity and that he really believed what he preached. Still others comment that the preacher showed a strong familiarity with the congregation; he spoke as one of them. In other words, the preacher had the smell of the sheep on him.

Among these comments collected over the years I have yet to hear someone praise a preacher because he was a great orator or an intellectual giant. To be sure, the preacher needs to be able to speak clearly and coherently, and he must have a good understanding of the Scripture and the tradition. But these students are listening for more. They are listening for a holy person, that is, someone who knows the Lord and believes that God is present with us.

Pope Francis talks about this experience of holiness in terms of "bearing witness." In a sermon for an ordination he exhorted the new priests, "May this be the nourishment of the People of God; . . . may your homilies touch the heart of the people because they come from your heart, because what you're telling them is what you carry in your heart." As Hippocrates admonished doctors to "First of all, do no harm," Francis warns preachers, "May your homilies not be boring."[4] In another homily, he charged, " 'One cannot understand a Christian without this witness' . . . Christianity is not a religion 'only of ideas, of pure theology, of aesthetics, of commandments. We are a people who follow Jesus Christ and bear witness, who want to bear witness to Jesus Christ.' "[5] The preacher must bear witness to Christ.

I can remember, shortly after my ordination, preaching an eight-day retreat with an elderly Jesuit priest. During the retreat he and I shared the duty of presiding and preaching at the daily Mass for the retreatants, alternating each day. At the time, he was in his seventies. He was a master of the Spiritual Exercises, having published much on the work of Ignatius of Loyola, and having directed many retreats. I knew I could learn much from him. But listening to him preach the first time surprised me. He had a very pronounced quiver in his voice that distracted me. I came to learn that, when he was a boy, he had suffered a bout of pneumonia. Because of this illness he had a lung removed, which caused the quiver in his voice. I decided, however, to concentrate on what he was saying rather than on how he sounded. His message was profound, unearthing new meaning from an old story and I could easily apply much of it to my own life. After a while I no longer noticed the quivering voice and the message came through loud and clear. I believe that this is the reason this priest proved to be a good preacher and spiritual director. The people who heard him regularly recognized him to be a holy man, who genuinely believed what he preached. So the preacher is one who is missioned by the church to spend time in prayer, reflecting on the word of God, as well as on the people who listen, in order to open the Scripture to those who are longing to see God's face.

Here is one final note about the preacher's stance. In listening to many preachers, eventually we may distinguish between two types: those who are "really preaching" and those who are "trying to preach." With those who are "really preaching," it is evident that they are well prepared and their expression is clear. They present their meaning in lucid language, which is accessible to the congregation, and the prose of the speech flows. They also exude a strong desire to communicate. It is as if they say, "Have I got a story to tell you!" And they hold our interest. More than this, we have the sense that they themselves are convinced by their message. Perhaps the greatest compliment a preacher may hear from a member of the congregation is, "You really believe what you said!" Whatever we think of it, whether we agree with these preachers or not, their sincerity and clarity urge us to listen. They are really preaching. In contrast, we sometimes hear from those who are trying to preach. They have done the preparation and have organized a sermon. But it may not be clear just what the preacher means to emphasize, or why we should accept it. Worse, we may wonder if the preacher really believes his own message. While it is all correct, is it convincing? We may have listened to an interesting subject, and perhaps it was illustrated by an amusing story, but was it preaching? Was the word of God opened for us today, moving us toward deeper discipleship?

Furthermore, we should ask, was the homily Christian? Let us pause here. Imagine that, through no fault of your own, you walk into church late for Mass, and you arrive just in time for the homily. From listening to the homily alone, would you know that you were in a Catholic Church? Would you know that the preacher is a Christian? Some of the preaching we hear presents good moral advice or sound psychological counseling. It is a message we might hear from Dr. Phil or from Oprah. It is good advice, to be sure, but is it a Christian message? Does it reveal the presence of Jesus Christ in our midst? Does it show us how the paschal mystery continues to unfold in our time? Does it remind us of how we are nourished regularly by the Lord's Body and Blood? And do we sense that the preacher really believes what has just been proclaimed? Did the preacher teach, move, and delight the congregation? Did the preacher name grace? In short, did we hear a Christian homily?

After a sufficient period of reflection, we are ready to move on to the next stage, to research.

CHAPTER SIX

Research: Mining the Text

For last year's words belong to last year's language
And next year's words await another voice.

—T. S. Eliot, *Little Gidding*

In the previous discussion on reflection we explained that the first question the preacher should ask when preparing to preach is, "What does the Scripture say to me?" rather than, "What can I say about the text?" As we prepare to research the material for preaching, a question to ask is, "What should I *not* say about this text?" This may seem a strange question to ask at the outset. However, consider that preaching involves interpretation in a two-part process. First, the preacher opens the meaning of the text from the ancient world—the world of the prophets and of the apostles. Second, the preacher applies that meaning to the modern world so that we learn how to live this message in our lives here and now. Since this is a matter of interpretation we need to be aware of our own bias. Each of us has a bias, that is, a particular way in which we view the world, a view that is influenced by our particular likes and dislikes, interests and ignorance, and all our experience in general. Each of us is biased; we cannot help that. Indeed, we should beware of the bias against bias, that is, the belief that we are completely free from bias. The best we can do is to be aware of our bias and not allow it to influence us unduly.

For example, I remember listening to a student preacher at a university ecumenical chapel service. The Scripture passage for the day told the story of Zacchaeus in the sycamore tree (Luke 19:1-10). The story is a familiar one, of how one day Jesus came to the town of Jericho. His reputation preceded him. Witnesses had told of miracle healings—he had recently cured a blind man— and of how he taught with compelling authority. The news of his visit spread and a large crowd came out to see him. Zacchaeus, a chief tax collector, stood among them. (He must have been successful as Luke tells us he was rich.) Unfortunately for him, though, he was rather short. Like a little boy trying to watch a parade at street level, jumping up and down, jostling back and forth, he tried to catch a glimpse of Jesus, but he could not see him. Finding a sycamore tree nearby, he climbed up into its wide-spreading branches and there he gained a commanding view of the street with a clear look at Jesus. And Jesus saw him. He stopped in his tracks and called to the little man sitting on the tree limb. "Zacchaeus, come down from there. I want to stay at your house." Zacchaeus felt overjoyed and jumped down to greet Jesus. But as the two of them walked together to his home, some people in the crowd were heard to murmur about Jesus, "He has gone to be the guest of one who is a sinner." Recall that tax collectors were considered to be dishonest, and were accused of cheating the Jewish people. What was especially despicable about their trade was that they were Jewish men employed by the Roman government to collect taxes from the Jews. It was also known that a number of them would inflate the tax fee so that they could keep a portion for themselves. The tax collectors were Jewish men cheating Jews while in the employ of the oppressive Roman government. Is it any wonder they were despised by the Jewish community, and their profession was ranked low, along with prostitutes?

Zacchaeus must have overheard this murmuring and he would have been aware of what others thought of him as a chief tax collector. So he turned to Jesus and assured him of his honesty, claiming that he contributes half of his earnings to the poor. Moreover, if he defrauded anyone he would repay that person with interest. Jesus must have been impressed with the little man, for he replied to him, "Today salvation has come to this house, because he too is a son of Abraham. For the Son of Man came to seek out and to save the lost." This is a summary of the story of Zacchaeus in the sycamore tree.

Back in the university chapel we listened attentively to the student preacher. His sermon did not bother to include any reference to Zacchaeus and his occupation. Instead he allowed his bias to direct the message. It was well known on campus that this young man was an avid environmentalist. He always spoke about the need to show care for the planet, which is certainly a noble cause. To all who would listen he would preach the gospel of good stewardship for the earth. Nevertheless, some of us were surprised when he brought this theme into the sermon. He chose to focus on Jesus calling a man down from the sycamore tree. He explained that by this action Jesus showed care for the tree, suggesting that the tax collector was abusing the tree by climbing it. He then went on to explain that we too should show care for trees and for all the living things that surround us. Now, I am sure that Jesus cared for trees, notwithstanding the time he cursed the fig tree, causing it to wither (Mark 11:12-25). However, this is not really the point of the story. Rather we hear once again, from Jesus' own lips, how he has come to search out and save those who are lost. In fact, immediately after this account he goes on to tell a parable in which he warns against those who judge others harshly (Luke 19:11-27).

We must be aware of our own bias. We are all biased in one way or another, and we should be aware of the bias and not let it direct our interpretation of the Scripture. We hear this bias on occasion with the preacher who always manages to steer the sermon toward a topic of personal interest, be it prayer, sexual morality, or social justice. To be sure, these are important issues and as members of the church, as well as of the larger society, we should be aware of them. However, when the preacher becomes predictable—always preaching on one or two topics—then the congregation may tune out (like the airline passengers mentioned earlier) and the preaching loses its effectiveness. So one reason why we engage in research is because the sources will tell us what we cannot say about the Scripture. The story of Zacchaeus is not about caring for trees. It is about the mercy of God who cares for all people.

To ask what we should not say about the text admittedly focuses on the negative. To speak more positively, during the prayerful preparation the preacher will discover an idea for preaching. This idea will then be confirmed and amplified by the commentators and other resources for research. For this discussion we will focus on the discipline of biblical criticism. Now, to be clear, by "criticism" we do not mean to speak negatively about something. Rather, "criticism" in this sense is taken from its Greek root, *kritikos*, meaning to analyze with careful judgment. To study something critically means to analyze it rather than casting a negative judgment about it. There are three methods of biblical criticism: literary, historical, and redaction. We will say a word about each.

The first method is literary criticism, which asks what type of literature characterizes this passage. Specifically we ask if the passage is historical, mythical, humorous, prophecy, or hyperbole. Was it written as a letter, such as an epistle? Or was it written as a hymn, a psalm, a poem, or a narrative? For example, some Christians choose to understand the story of creation in the book of Genesis as a historical account, reading literally that the creation of the universe was completed in precisely six days, with the Lord resting on the seventh day. Others will read this passage as a mythical account, one that reveals a profound truth through a story. By the way, the word "myth" suffers a bad reputation in our culture. It is often misused, suggesting that it means fiction or simply a lie. On the contrary, mythic stories are attempts to explain creation and divinity, as well as the meaning of our existence, and they do so by telling a story. So when my students ask if the story of Adam and Eve is true, I answer "yes." Then I explain that it is true, although not in a scientific or historical sense. I do not believe that there was a "Mr." Adam and a "Ms." Eve who conceived the chain of humanity. But the story is true in a moral sense. We learn an important moral truth from the story of Adam and Eve, namely, that almighty God created the universe and formed human beings in his own image and likeness. We also learn that pride perverts human relationships by allowing us to see ourselves as superior to others. We too may be seduced by the serpent's empty promise, "You can be like God!" Pride is the root of all evil. According to most Scripture scholars we miss the meaning of the first two chapters of the book of Genesis if we interpret them historically. Rather, through an appreciation of myth we may glean the moral truth. So one question we ask about the passage is, what type of literature is it? This will influence our understanding of the message.

A second method of biblical criticism is historical. Here we inquire into the historical period in which this episode occurred.

What do we need to know about the culture, customs, and language of the period that may shed light on the passage? We work to explore the mind-set of the people of that era. For example, St. Mark records a scene in his gospel in which Jesus discovers that the apostles have been arguing among themselves about who is the greatest (Mark 9:33-37). In response he tells them that, if they want to be considered great in the eyes of God, they will have to become servants. Then, to illustrate the point, Jesus picks up a child and holds him up in front of them. He tells them that they must become like this child. In a twenty-first-century mind-set we might think that Jesus' action is rather cute or sentimental. Following this line of thought we might think it would be helpful if we could, somehow, maintain some of our childlike dreams and views of the world. After all, our children are the hope for the future. We might think this way. However, people living in the first century would have a different understanding of Jesus' action because they regarded children differently. According to Scripture scholar Daniel Harrington, in Jesus' day children had no rights. In the eyes of the law they were nonpersons. Also, children were totally dependent upon their parents, who did not have much to gain from them, either socially or financially. Moreover, the Greek word used in this passage, *talya,* could refer either to a child or a servant. There is nothing "cute" in Jesus holding up the child; rather, it is a radical call to humility.

The third method of biblical criticism is redaction criticism. Here we take note of the way the editors arranged their material, that is, which material they include or exclude, and how it is organized throughout the book. Let us focus on the gospels. Redaction criticism helps us to understand the three Synoptic Gospels, Mark, Matthew, and Luke. A careful reading of these three shows many similarities. Also, the standard two-source theory indicates that both Matthew and Luke borrowed material from Mark. Yet Matthew and Luke also differ in their telling of the life, death, and resurrection of Jesus, along with the growth of the early church. Thus it is believed that Matthew and Luke each had their own sources.

Looking at these gospels through a focus on the work of the editor will reveal more of the meaning of the Christian tradition. For example, consider the lesson of the Beatitudes, which we find in both Matthew and Luke. Matthew's version is probably better known since he gives us the familiar account of the "Sermon on the Mount" with eight beatitudes delivered on a hilltop. In contrast, Luke recounts four beatitudes and four "woes," or threats, and Jesus delivers these on a plain. To appreciate the difference we need to inquire about the audience to whom each evangelist is writing. As we mentioned earlier, the first rule of public speaking is to know your audience. We might say the same for the writer. The evangelists are writing to particular communities of Christians. Each community has its own cultural context as well as a set of questions and concerns.

Matthew, for instance, writes to a community of Jewish Christians. Much like the apostles, these people have been raised in Jewish culture. They would have celebrated regularly the feasts of Passover and Pentecost, and they would have remembered their history as told through the stories of the patriarchs and the prophets. And they would keep the commandments as given them by their liberator, Moses. For the faithful Jew, the story of Jesus ascending the mount to proclaim the Beatitudes would resonate with memories of Moses atop Mount Sinai. The Jewish Christians came to see Jesus as the new Moses. In contrast, Luke's community consists of Gentile Christians. They are mostly of Greek heritage, so Jewish culture would be foreign to them. They did not revere Moses as a religious figure, nor did they follow the Ten Commandments received on the mount. But one of the themes running through the Gospel of Luke is that of Jesus as the champion of the poor and lowly, the *anawim*. Luke situates this episode on a plain. (His version is known as the "Sermon on the Plain.") That plain, a low-lying area, is more accessible to people who are sick or handicapped. This is where Jesus meets the crowd of followers. The questions posed by redaction criticism help to uncover details of the Bible and aid us in telling the story of salvation.

The critical analysis of the Scripture provides the preacher with a means for "mining the text." Before looking for stories or analogies or jokes to make the biblical message relevant or palatable, we need to dig deep into the story. Our Scripture is a classical work and we never exhaust its meaning. As we learn more of the ancient world, its language and customs, and strive to apply it to our world, we uncover fresh meaning and may reveal grace around us.

Finally, for the task of research, preachers are fortunate to have many resources at their disposal. Here are just a few. I recommend for the preacher's bookshelf a one-volume commentary such as *The New Jerome Biblical Commentary* and *The New Interpreter's Study Bible*. Both volumes contain concise articles for each book of the Bible as well as topics in general. For more in-depth study, consult a commentary series, such as the *Anchor Bible*, or *Sacra Pagina*. (A Christian university library will most likely have them on the shelf. Hopefully the local library will have them available as well.) Also, a good Bible dictionary is helpful to explore specific topics in greater depth. I recommend *Dictionary of the Bible*, by John L. McKenzie, SJ, and *The Oxford Companion to the Bible*, edited by Bruce Metzger and Michael Coogan. A map of the Holy Land will help provide a picture of the setting for the Scripture story. There are also good homily services on the web, for example, Preacher Exchange. At this site you will find a weekly article, "First Impressions" by Fr. Jude Siciliano, OP. This is not a homily but "impressions" or ideas that will be helpful in thinking about the homily. In contrast, I am wary of using the prepared homilies that can be found on the web as well as in print. To take them from the page to the pulpit may violate the orator's principle, "know your audience." We need to ask, will this general homily be appropriate—will it sound relevant—to my specific congregation? To be sure, we may glean ideas from the homily service and use them for our own preparation without bringing the text into the pulpit.

Having prayed with the Scripture passages and conducted our research, we are ready for the third phase of preparation—to write the homily.

CHAPTER SEVEN

Write: Mapping the Homily

Find a subject you care about.
Do not ramble, though.
Keep it simple.
Have the guts to cut.
Sound like yourself.
Say what you mean to say.
Pity the readers.

—Kurt Vonnegut

It helps to write out the homily, even if we do not take the manuscript into the pulpit. Writing helps to give direction to our thoughts and expression to our ideas. The written text gives direction in that we have a beginning, a middle, and an end. In other words, we know how to begin the homily, how to develop a coherent idea, and then how to conclude the message. The text becomes a map to guide the preacher and later to lead the listener. The exercise of writing gives us the chance to reflect, so that we can choose the proper wording and, most importantly, learn what it is we really want to say. (Occasionally a student will answer in class, "I know it but I can't explain it." Let's be honest: If we cannot explain it, then we really don't know it. We may have an inkling of what we mean, but we really cannot say we understand it.) Writing out the homily provides an opportunity to clarify our thoughts and express ourselves clearly. The written text should answer two questions. First, what do I want to say? And second, what is the best way to say it?

Someone advised that writing a speech takes four drafts. The first draft is simply to get the ideas down, either on paper or on the computer screen. For this draft the writer simply spews out ideas, jots down words, draws an outline, and sketches the homily. Meanwhile the internal censor is kept mute; the critical evaluation will come later. To be sure, much of what we write will be thrown out or altered, but for the first draft, just get it down—start writing. Begin to write even if you have nothing to write. The US bishops note in *Fulfilled in Your Hearing* that sometimes preachers sit down to write without having any idea of what they are going to say. They may feel empty and uninspired. The bishops advise, "Begin writing anyway, for the very act of writing often unleashes a flow of ideas that will be new, fresh and exciting."[1]

In the second draft, add words, images, and quotations, filling out the text for clarification. Also, now we can craft the sentences, shape the paragraphs, and scan the word choice. In the third draft, we comb through the text, omitting unnecessary words, images, and examples. The great jazz musician Miles Davis said, "I always listen to what I can leave out." For Davis, an important part of his music was to know which notes *not* to play. Here Davis echoes Kurt Vonnegut, who is quoted above, "Have the guts to cut."

Vonnegut also advises the writer, "Sound like yourself." This is easier said than done. In my students' writing they use the passive voice all too often, along with sophisticated wording to express simple ideas. They think this sounds more mature or professional. However, in writing it helps to "keep it simple." Ask yourself, Would you use this word regularly in speaking with others? Does this sound like you? To quote Miles Davis again, "Sometimes you have to play a long time to be able to play like yourself." The same can be said for the preacher: It takes a long time until you find your voice. If the preacher is going to "delight" the listeners, following Augustine's model, by which the preacher inspires the listeners and they have the strong sense that the preacher is talking to them, then they will need to know that he is genuine, and so he needs to sound genuine.

The congregation will judge if the preacher has prepared well. Many of those sitting in the pews listen regularly to speeches, lectures, sales pitches, and advertising. They will decide if they think the preacher, first of all, knows what he is talking about, and if he truly cares about the subject and about them. More than this, a well-prepared homily shows care and respect for the congregation—like the dinner invitation to someone's home, where the host takes the time to set an attractive table, prepares a savory and satisfying meal, and then allows time for the guests to linger. All this preparation shows care for the guests. When the preacher takes time to craft the homily with prayerfulness, research, and style, the people may glimpse the care of the Lord for them. As mentioned earlier, the people of God are not so much looking for a brilliant theologian or a seasoned thespian. Rather, they are listening for a holy person, one who knows the Christian story and can tell it with clarity and conviction.

A written text is also practical because it helps us to keep track of the time. Depending on the congregation and the occasion, the length of the homily will vary. For a Sunday liturgy I figure on preaching eight to ten minutes, but some congregations will expect a longer homily—again, it is important to know your audience. Writing out the homily is one way to ensure that we will not ramble at the ambo. We will not get caught searching for a word or an illustration, or worry over what comes next.

Finally, if you bring the manuscript into the ambo, it helps to format it in a user-friendly way, that is, in a way that is easy to read. On a computer you can do this with font size, spacing, and sense lines. I like to read the text without my eyeglasses, so I use a sixteen-point font with double-spacing between lines. I also type the text in sense lines, similar to the way that the Lectionary presents the Scripture texts. This format makes it easy to glance down at the page, grasp a phrase or a sentence, and look up again to speak. It also makes it less likely that I will lose my place on the page. Of course, there is no substitute for being familiar with the text, so we will not look as if we are glued to it. Be sure to number the pages just in case they get mixed up. Print on one side of the paper only, making it easy to slide a page across when you finish reading it. For this reason, too, do not staple the pages together.

These are some general points to consider when sitting down to write. One of the more specific points is that the preacher needs to have a clear idea of what he means to say if he is to teach, delight, and move the congregation. We will look at this now.

The Structure of the Homily

Having a structure for the homily is essential to presenting a clear message. The structure provides a map to guide the listeners along and to keep the preacher on track. For a model of a structure we can refer to Augustine again. In *De Doctrina Christiana*, he addressed both the theory and practice of preaching. Earlier we discussed his idea of a threefold purpose of preaching. He also provides a threefold structure for composing the homily. Augustine urges preachers to employ the art of rhetoric so that, in his words, "they may know how to make their listeners benevolent, or attentive, or docile, in their presentation" (4.2.3). I remember a debate coach instructing his young orators, "Make your speech b-a-d," that is, structure the speech so that it is heard as benevolent, attentive, and docile.

To illustrate the point, picture a political candidate attending a rally as she is trying to drum up votes. She walks briskly onto the stage, and begins her stump speech with a few kind words for this town and a word of gratitude for all those who went out of their way to attend the rally. She then launches into an agenda with a litany of concerns facing these folks today. It is clear she has done her homework; she knows these people and she knows their needs. She will then suggest some solutions, offering a practical plan to improve their lives. Finally, she hopes to influence them to see that she is the one who can solve their problems and lead them to a better future—and that is why they should vote for her come election day. In a simple way she has followed Augustine's method of rendering the audience benevolent, attentive, and docile. Now let's say a word about each of these steps.

The speaker begins by rendering the audience benevolent (from the Latin *bene vole*, meaning "good will"). The speaker wants to show that he is one with the audience. Remember the earlier discussion on where the preacher stands in relation to the congregation. It is important to establish a proper balance between the pulpit and the pew. It is not good for the speaker to appear too familiar or "folksy." Nor should he tower above the assembly, in a position of superiority, even if he is standing in a pulpit. The question is, how will the preacher introduce the message in a way that is interesting and accessible?

In Arthur Miller's play *The Crucible*, John Proctor challenges the pastor of his Salem church for his fire-and-brimstone preaching. Reverend Parris has just pronounced in his sermon, "There is either obedience or the church will burn like Hell is burning!" To which Proctor complains, "I have trouble enough without I come five miles to hear him preach only hellfire and bloody damnation. Take it to heart, Mr. Parris. There are many others who stay away from church these days because you hardly ever mention God any more."[2]

For the introduction of the homily, will the preacher begin with the image of God or the fall of humanity? Christians believe that human beings are created in the image and likeness of God. We also believe that human nature has been corrupted through the sin of pride. What does the preacher use for a starting point—the image of God or the fall of humanity?

Some preachers like to begin by focusing on a current social problem or an issue of popular culture. During the season of Advent, for example, we are sure to hear from the pulpit some criticism of how the season has become commercialized. The criticism will be followed by a plea to "keep Christ in Christmas." The commercialization of Christmas is a concern, especially given the expanding secular society. However, would it prove more effective to lead from a positive point of view, that is to say, for the preacher to remind the assembly of the reason for the celebration and why almighty God chose to dwell with us? As discussed earlier, God freely chose to tell his story through Jesus Christ, the living Word of God, so that we would come to know him. From this story we learn of the God of surprises. Instead of arriving in royal splendor, Mary gives birth to her son in a stable.

The story of Christ's birth is countercultural. It challenges the status quo and reverses the values of the world. Recall King Herod's jealous rage when he was threatened by rumors of a newborn king, and how his rage led to the slaughter of the innocents. A rich and powerful king was deeply disturbed by news of a baby's birth. Recall also Mary's jubilation because God had called upon this lowly handmaid to bear his word. The annunciation to Mary follows a pattern found throughout the gospels—a pattern of call and sending. Before the Lord sends any of his followers on a mission he first calls them, taking time to teach them. He reminds them of who he is for them, and that he calls them into a closer relationship with himself. The preacher should preach like Jesus did, calling the faithful back to Christ, making clear where they stand with the Lord, before laying out their mission.

Clearly the preacher needs to address the problems of the day for the particular community, whether they are spiritual or social. For example, how will we handle the growing secularization of our society and the new aggressive atheism that threatens religious freedom? How should the church address the racial tension still prevalent in our cities, and the plight of refugees throughout the world? These and other issues do need to be addressed. Here is today's harvest, ready to be reaped, and the Lord still looks for laborers who are ready and willing to serve. There are real concerns for the church, and the preacher may help to raise consciousness about them, and then challenge the people, directing them to pastoral action.

Along the way, the preacher will want to avoid several pitfalls. First of all, are the concerns of the preacher real concerns for the assembly? For example, I can remember concelebrating a liturgy on Holy Thursday, which that year just happened to fall on April 1. The preacher saw a problem with the coincidence of the foot washing and April Fools' Day. He seemed to think that much of society would be absorbed in the antics of the day, while we serious Christians focused on the "love command" of Jesus Christ. However, was this a real concern? Were the faithful in that church truly distracted by April Fools? It seemed to be an issue for the preacher alone. In general, we hear with some regularity how preachers attack some aspects of popular culture, like a controversial movie, a racy hit song, or the scandalous behavior of a celebrity. But will this concern bear weight in the pulpit or will it float away, having been dismissed by the listeners who think it is simply the preacher's pet peeve?

Second, it is better to speak in support of something rather than to go on the attack. If I intend to preach against something there is the possibility that the issue itself, rather than the gospel, will come to define my homily. For example, in addressing the problem of abortion and speaking in the name of the church, it would be helpful to focus on the dignity of human life and the need to protect the innocent. Then, within this context, the problem of abortion should be addressed. In this way we maintain focus on our goal of human dignity . . . because we are created in the image and likeness of God.

Third, beware of the litany of woes. Some preachers like to remind us of the bleak world in which we live. They will recite a list of crises, culled from the daily news reports. This list is then followed by a plea to place our trust in God. There is a problem, though, when the preacher spends much time and energy on the problem, but little effort on the solution or our salvation. We have the sense that the preacher was more interested in—indeed energized by—the dark news, but he provided little light to help us see the way through. Sometimes the long litany of woes becomes debilitating and the meager dose of hope provides little cure. What does the preacher intend for the assembly to remember: the agony of a fallen world, or the ecstasy of the Lord's salvation?

Having rendered the audience benevolent, the speaker then strives to render them attentive. Here the fruit of reflection and research comes to bear. The speaker proves he is well informed. In this moment the preacher "teaches"—not turning the pulpit into a lecturer's podium, but deepening the congregation's understanding of the Christian tradition. The preacher draws upon the familiar, building upon what they already know. The preacher will discuss ideas gleaned from biblical criticism to flesh out new meaning from an old text. The history of that particular era, or the situation of the people in the passage and the author's purpose in writing to them, or a technical term translated from Greek or Hebrew—all help to bring the story to life. The faithful come to appreciate that this is their story, rather than just another story.

Finally, when the speaker has succeeded in rendering the audience both benevolent and attentive, he then moves on to the final step: rendering them docile. Some wince when they hear the word "docile" in this context, as it seems to suggest sheep-like behavior, or simply having a calming effect. However, literally speaking, "docile" is rooted in the Latin word *docilis*, meaning "readily taught." Having been rendered attentive, the audience now asks, "What's next? Where do we go from here? How do we put into action what we have just learned?" This is when the preacher leads the listeners. He may lead them to more fervent prayer, to works of charity, or to a social justice response. Good preaching should also lead us to the table of the Eucharist, where we are united with Jesus Christ in that most profound way, as he personally directed his followers, saying, "Do this in memory of me."

The structure of the homily will help to move the congregation along; it also keeps the preacher focused. Generally speaking, some preachers like to begin with a story to illustrate the lesson and then move into the meaning of the Scripture. For many preachers this is effective. However, as Bishop Krister Stendahl, an eminent New Testament scholar, once warned, sometimes the congregation will remember the story but forget the gospel. One problem is that the story can be presented vividly with clear images and an enthusiastic tone. And then the gospel is presented like a dry lecture. Sometimes the preacher shows more interest in his own story than in the gospel. To be clear, it can be helpful to use a non-scriptural story to illustrate the Scripture of the day. The question to ask is, which story will the congregation remember? If they remember your story but not the story of Jesus Christ, then you have failed. But if they leave church with a deeper understanding of their relationship with Christ because the story shed light on the Scripture, then you have preached well.

Make Your Sermon Portable

There is an old adage among preachers: "Make your sermon portable so that the people can carry it home." In other words, what do you want the congregation to remember? If they remember just one point or one image or one idea from your preaching, what should it be? What will they carry home with them? The challenge is for the preacher to ensure that the listeners will leave with this point etched in their minds and pulsing in their hearts.

So, after writing out the homily, the preacher should have a clear idea of this message and should be able to state it in one or two sentences. As the saying goes, "If there's a mist in the pulpit, there will be a fog in the pew." This is to say that if the message is not crystal clear to the preacher, the listeners will find the meaning quite fuzzy. To remedy this, the preacher may simply state the point to be remembered, as a teacher sometimes will say to a class, "If you remember nothing else, this is what I want you to remember today."

Or, the preacher may repeat the line that the congregation should carry home. This line could then become a refrain throughout the homily, making it easy to remember. (Think of a pop song with a catchy refrain, the one you can't seem to get out of your head.) For example, how do we remember the speech delivered by Dr. Martin Luther King Jr. at the Lincoln Memorial in August of 1963? We refer to it as his "I have a dream" speech because King used this line as a refrain. We can imagine that the audience left Washington, DC, that day, repeating the phrase, "I have a dream."

The lesson to be stressed here is that the homily should have one clear point. In structuring the text, everything within the homily should point to this message. For this reason it helps to have just one illustration or example. Using more than one can make the homily appear to be like a cluttered gallery with too many paintings, making it hard to focus on any one work of art. Too many illustrations becomes a distraction. Use one, and present it clearly.

One problem we often encounter in preparing the homily is finding that we have two or more good stories or illustrations to use. Each one of them is appropriate for the message, and is interesting, and entertaining, and we are loath to cut them. But taken together, will they help to move the homily along, or will they leave the listeners baffled? Let's return to the dinner table for an example. In planning a dinner party, you probably would not serve pasta, potatoes, and rice in the same meal. Each one of them is good, but usually one starch is enough for a meal. Likewise, beware of filling up on the illustrations and losing the focus of the message. Here, it would help to remember the violent advice for writers, attributed to William Faulkner, "In writing, you must kill your darlings." He means to make us aware of the writer who employs personal favorites that do not enhance the story. We can apply the rule to preaching. The darlings may hold special meaning for the preacher, but they may distract the congregation.

Along with this, I find it helpful, as a rule, to throw away the first page of my draft. While the first page was necessary to begin the writing process, it sometimes becomes superfluous to the homily. The first page may be the "icebreaker"; it was useful to get the conversation started. It contains the first impressions or the first thoughts and images that came to mind when beginning to write the homily. They were important, then. But do I need them now? For example, does it help to tell us how you prepared to preach on this occasion? In this first page we often hear how the preacher prepared for this homily; is this necessary? Another standard line from the "first page" is how the readings for today are either so difficult or seem inappropriate for today's celebration, yet the preacher is stuck with them. (For some preachers, this has become their usual introduction.) In a normal conversation, we sometimes need to talk for a while, developing our thoughts, before we land on what we mean to say. The same is true for this "conversation," the homily. But the preacher has the opportunity to edit the conversation beforehand so that the listeners will remain focused. The attentive listeners weave together the threads of a speech, connecting them in their minds. If they find too many "loose threads"—threads of thought that seem to have no purpose—the listeners may find it a futile effort and drift away into a daydream. Again, what will the congregation carry home with them?

Furthermore, think of the great literature you have read and the memorable movies you have seen. They do not all begin with "Once upon a time" or "It was a dark and stormy night." Dickens begins *A Tale of Two Cities* with "It was the best of times, it was the worst of times . . ." Tolstoy begins *Anna Karenina* with "All happy families are alike; each unhappy family is unhappy in its own way." Remember the opening scene of *The Godfather* with Don Corleone seated in a dark room receiving guests who have come to request favors from him. And in the film *Forrest Gump* we see Gump seated at a bus stop while a floating leaf falls from a tree and lands right by his feet. These opening lines and scenes give us a glimpse of what is to come. The introduction is designed to bring us swiftly into the plot. In short, throw away the first page in order to move the story along.

Finally, when all is said and done, that is, when reading over a draft of the homily, the preacher should ask, "So what?" Let us presume for now that the text is well written, and that it has been thoroughly researched, and that it will be delivered in an engaging manner. Nevertheless, what difference will it make when the congregation hears this message? The question of "so what" should challenge the preacher to engage more with the message. How has the preacher been moved by the Scripture that will be proclaimed within the cultural context of this congregation? Preachers need to know the difference it makes to themselves before announcing the difference it will make to their listeners.

For example, consider the Easter homily. While all preaching tests the faith of the preacher, preaching on Easter Sunday presents a special challenge. On this holiest of days we have to contend with the question of what we really believe about the paschal mystery and the resurrection of Jesus Christ. We need to ask, just what is the relevance—the good news—of the resurrection for us today? Indeed, we know what happened; it is a familiar story. But why should this first-century story be relevant for Christians—or for anyone—in the twenty-first century? What is its meaning for the citizens of a consumer society, who are driven by technology and go racing along at a furious pace? How will we make the good news of Christ's resurrection relevant for the modern world? Jesus Christ has risen from the dead, alleluia! . . . So what?

I can remember teaching a class of prep school freshmen; it was an enjoyable class. The topic for the day was the resurrection of Jesus Christ. In trying to explain the meaning of the resurrection one phrase came tripping off my tongue, and I tried to deliver it in a professorial tone: "Because of Christ's resurrection, death is but a doorway to eternal life." I remember feeling proud of myself for uttering this phrase. But as I looked around the classroom I watched the boys, presumably scribbling down the phrase in their notebooks, with the same interest as if the teacher had recited a rule of grammar or a theorem of geometry. Somehow I had expected more of a personal response from them. When I mentioned my disappointment to my chairman he replied, "Maybe it is because you taught it like a rule of grammar or a theorem of geometry." That small incident forced me to reflect upon my faith in the paschal mystery. Indeed, what does the resurrection mean for the followers of Jesus Christ today?

Humor

Can humor help a homily? Is there a place for levity in preaching? There is definitely a place for humor in the pulpit. Humor is an essential component of the human condition. Laughter has a way of lightening our load and carrying us along. "Laugh and the world laughs with you," as the saying goes. And laughter can help bond the preacher with the listeners.

For an inspiring and entertaining discussion of holiness and humor I recommend the book *Between Heaven and Mirth*, by Fr. James Martin. In this book Martin quotes Cardinal Walter Kasper, a well-respected theologian who argues for the role of humor in the church today. Kasper says, "The lack of humor and irritability into which we in the contemporary church and contemporary theology have so often slipped is perhaps one of the most serious objections which can be brought against present-day Christians."[3]

Humor is an expression of our humanity and humility. We laugh not only at jokes but also when we hear a surprise ending, or when the underdog finishes on top. The disciples must have laughed when they realized the good news of the resurrection: Jesus is alive! He has risen from the dead! There is no way they could have expected this. As Martin says, God introduced joy, humor, and laughter into even the most serious of situations. Recall the story of Abraham and Sarah, longing for the child promised to them by God. There was the faithful "Father of Nations," in his twilight years, still awaiting a child. And one day God spoke to Abraham and assured him that soon Sarah would bear a child. God said, " 'I will bless [Sarah], and moreover I will give you a son by her. I will bless her, and she shall give rise to nations; kings of peoples shall come from her.' Then Abraham fell on his face and laughed" (Gen 17:16-17). Abraham then went home and told Sarah the good yet shocking news, that soon she would be a mother. And "Sarah laughed to herself." Sometime later their son was born and they named him—what else?—Isaac, a Hebrew word meaning "he laughs." The God of surprises sometimes amuses us. This amusement is the "delight" Augustine describes in his purpose of preaching.

So how can we use humor in our preaching? Someone advised that the first rule of humor in public speaking should be, If you are naturally funny, use it; if not, don't. Humor can contribute much to a speech and to a homily. However, it can be painful to listen to a speaker who is trying to be funny but cannot convey the humorous point. A comic knows how to set up a story, leading to a surprise ending (something we did not see coming), and has the proper timing to carry the audience to the finish. The comic observations of Jerry Seinfeld and Paula Poundstone are good examples of this craft. Humor can be very helpful in a speech, carrying the audience along and revealing an insight.

For the preacher laughter can be a signal that the congregation is receptive to the message. However, let us pause here to ask, receptive to what? Is the congregation receptive to the preaching or to the preacher? Are they focused upon the message or the messenger? Some preachers feel the need to entertain. This may be because they very much want to be liked. Some preachers need the affection and adulation of the crowd, so humor becomes an attempt to claim the attention they so crave. Others display a fundamental distrust for the liturgy. They find worship stuffy and rigid, so they try to loosen things up and make it more personal so that they feel comfortable. The result is to take the focus off of Christ and place it on themselves. It is as if they say, "You have heard *Jesus* tell you . . . but now *I* tell you . . ." In the end, whose message will we remember?

Further, while humor may be helpful for an effective speech, the preacher should avoid jokes. For one reason, what happens if the joke fails and people do not laugh? Either the listeners did not understand the joke or just did not think it was funny. How will the preacher recover? Johnny Carson, the king of the late night talk show, was masterful at recovering from the jokes that bombed in his monologue. That was a skill honed after many years onstage. However, with many preachers, the failed joke leaves the congregation in a painful state, worrying how the preacher will recover and wondering if they can trust the preacher. Moreover, even if the joke succeeds and the people laugh, then what? What will follow? How does the joke connect with the message of the good news for today? The preacher has just spent one minute to set up and deliver a joke, and then pause for laughter. Given the ten-minute homily, as discussed earlier, this is a considerable amount of time. Moreover, does the joke provide direction or is it a distraction?

Nevertheless, using jokes must be fairly common for Catholic preachers. I am often asked to recommend books with collections of jokes that are appropriate for preaching. This seems to presume that every preacher tells jokes. However, I learned a lesson from comic playwright Neil Simon. He wrote the plays *The Odd Couple*, *Plaza Suite*, *Broadway Bound*, and many more. In an interview on *Inside the Actors Studio* with James Lipton, Simon was asked, "How do you write your jokes?" He answered, "I don't write jokes." He went on to explain that he writes situations for his characters in which the audience may recognize themselves, and when they do, they laugh. Telling stories with a humorous twist can be much more effective than joke telling. The story plays a part in conveying the message. It moves in the same direction rather than being a distraction. Also, even if the listeners do not find the story particularly funny, the preacher can continue with the story because it serves as an illustration for the message.

Furthermore, the rush to a book of jokes is similar to seeking out some story to match the gospel for the day. This brings us back to the topic of "mining the text." Before adding a joke or a funny anecdote, have we considered the possibility of finding a humorous shard encased in the Scripture text? Believe it or not, the Bible is a fairly funny book. This is to say that there is a good amount of humor to be found among the many Bible stories. Clearly, biblical passages may not sound all that humorous to us. However, as we mine the text looking through the lens of literary criticism, we find that some passages need to be understood in a lighthearted, rather than a literal, vein.

Let's look at two stories, one from the New Testament and one from the Old Testament. Recall the gospel parable when Jesus stands before a crowd of people and says to them, "Is there anyone among you who, if your child asks for a fish, will give a snake instead of a fish? Or if the child asks for an egg, will give a scorpion?" (Luke 11:11-12). The parable provides a lively and humorous instruction on prayer. Try to picture the scene, perhaps engaging in a contemplation of place, as discussed earlier. See the crowd gathered around Jesus. Imagine the reactions of the people to Jesus. It would be silly to imagine that this crowd mulled over Jesus' questions, as if they had to think about the answer. It should be obvious: no decent parents who love their children would do, or even think of, such a thing. Now, imagine Jesus asking this in a light-hearted way, already knowing the answer. See the crowd of people—many of them fathers and mothers with children in tow—chuckling at such an outrageous thought. They recognize themselves in the moment because they know they could never deny or deceive their children in such a way. The ripples of laughter move their hearts closer to the speaker, opening them to the message. Then he tells them, Well, if you fathers and mothers cannot refuse your own children, and you are far from perfect, how much more will your heavenly Father do for you, if only you would ask?

Brendan Byrne writes in his commentary *The Hospitality of God*, "The genius of the parable . . . is that it engages intense human feeling (the sense of shame; the sense of parental love and responsibility) and draws these directly into an attitude toward God. Jesus does not *tell* his hearers about God. He makes them *feel* something very deeply and then says, 'That—multiplied a thousand and more times over—is how God feels about you! It is in the light of this knowledge that you should come before God in prayer.'"[4]

For still another story, listen to the account of Abraham, as he bargains with God, trying to save the town of Sodom, as told in the book of Genesis, 18:16-33. How do you hear this conversation? One day, after reading this passage a few times, I imagined Abraham as the TV detective Columbo, played by the actor Peter Falk. Homicide detective Lieutenant Columbo had a way of appearing naïve. Wearing a rumpled trench coat and chomping on a short cigar, he would badger his suspects with so many questions until they would finally submit and confess to the crime. They had been deceived by his simplistic style. So here is Abraham, sounding ever so humble and reverent, addressing God with utmost respect, yet he is persistent in his goal. He is sly and he gets his way. We learn from this story about the relationship between God the Father and Israel, and how God is moved genuinely by his people.

These two stories are examples of how, through literary criticism and our own imagination, we may find humor in the Scripture text. And leave the joke books in the recreation room.

"What's Love Got to Do with It?"

The word "love" is heard in so many homilies that some may wonder if the word has lost its meaning. I suggest that we should not use the word unless it appears in the Scripture of the day. Indeed love is good, and love is of God, but the word is overused in popular culture and in preaching. Think of all the pop songs singing about love. When all is said and done, "love" has been reduced to a good feeling, or an emotional high.

In a way one could say that all preaching is about love, that is, that the love of God for humanity is displayed through the paschal mystery. And the praise of God in worship along with the works of charity display the love for God by the faithful. Saint John wrote, "God is love, and those who abide in love abide in God, and God abides in them" (1 John 4:16). When preaching on this Scripture verse Pope Francis commented, "This word 'love' is a word that is used so many times and when we use it we don't know exactly what it means. What is love?" He went on to say that some people think of real love as what we see in soap operas or the feeling we get when we have a crush on someone. But that feeling eventually fades away. The pope then asks, where do we find the true source of love? And he answers, "Whoever loves has been created by God because God is love." He also warns us to beware of saying, "Every love is [of] God. No, God is love."[5] God is the One who loved us first.

In preaching, it would help to have the word "love" opened in order to mine the depth of its meaning. There is a difference between sentimental and sacramental love. On the one hand, sentimental love makes us feel good about ourselves. After all, who doesn't want to be loved? On the other hand, sacramental love is transformative, changing us and bringing us closer to the presence of God. It also requires sacrifice.

So what are we talking about when we talk about love? C. S. Lewis wrote about several different types of love in his book *The Four Loves*. The first type of love he describes is *storge*, which is a bond of empathy between those who are brought together by chance as, for example, the love between a mother and her child. This love is expressed as both a need and a gift. The second type of love is *philia*, the bond of friendship shared by people with common interests, values, and activities. The third type is *eros*, the erotic bond experienced by two people in love. For Lewis, *eros* should not be confused with what we hear of today as "erotica," that is, raw sexuality related to promiscuity. Lewis makes a clear distinction. With *eros* we find a man who desires one particular woman and he is passionate for her; with "erotica" we find a man who wants any woman. The fourth type of love is *agape*, which is unconditional love. This love is willing to serve other people regardless of changing circumstances. For Lewis, *agape* is the love of God.

We can find a play on two of these words in the Gospel of John (21:1-19). Here we find a dialogue between Jesus and Peter. In the English translation this dialogue is normally read as Jesus asking Peter, "Do you love me?" And Peter responding, "Yes, Lord, you know I love you." However, a look into the Greek text reveals new meaning. Jesus asks, "Peter, do you *agape* me?" And Peter replies, "Yes, Lord, I *philia* you." It is as if Jesus asks Peter, are you willing to sacrifice yourself for me? And Peter answers, "I am willing to be your friend." The second time Jesus asks, "Do you *agape* me?" And again Peter replies, "Lord, I *philia* you." But the third time, Jesus asks, "Do you *philia* me?" And Peter says, a little indignantly, "Lord, you know everything. You know I *philia* you." Jesus meets Peter on his own terms. Maybe Peter just wasn't ready to make that commitment. Jesus did not condemn or abandon his disciple. Instead he left him with an ominous message: "[Someday,] someone else will . . . take you where you do not wish to go." Jesus forgave Peter and he did prove himself eventually. We know that in the end Peter did lose his life because he could not stop preaching Jesus' name. In the end he was able to say, "Yes, Lord, I *agape* you."

This digression into Lewis's *Four Loves* is simply to help us reflect upon the meaning of the word "love." The preacher needs to define the word lest it lose its meaning. Leo Tolstoy wrote, in *Anna Karenina*, "Love . . . The reason I dislike that word is that it means too much for me, far more than you can understand."[6] And Fyodor Dostoevsky wrote in *The Brothers Karamazov*, "Love in action is a harsh and dreadful thing compared with love in dreams."[7] And Jesus said, "No one has greater love than this, to lay down one's life for one's friends" (John 15:13).

Pope Francis addressed the question of the meaning of love in his apostolic exhortation *Amoris Laetitia*, The Joy of Love (2016). In the chapter titled "Love in Marriage," he offers the excerpt from St. Paul's First Letter to the Corinthians (13:4-7) as a description of love. According to the pope, "In a lyrical passage of Saint Paul, we see some of the features of true love" (90). Paul writes that love is patient and kind, never jealous or boastful, neither arrogant nor rude. Love does not insult. It is not irritable or resentful, and does not rejoice at wrong, but rejoices in the right. Love bears all things, hopes all things, endures all things. The pope goes on to comment on each one of these features of love. Notice that according to St. Paul love is not a feeling. Rather love is a decision to live for, and to seek union with, another.

So just what are we talking about when we talk about love? Love is beautiful yet quite complicated. It is comforting to know that God is love. And it is challenging to be asked to abide in God's love. We need to hear from the preacher how God loves us and how we may abide in this love. In short, "All You Need Is Love" may be a good title for a pop song, but a bad theme for a sermon.

CHAPTER EIGHT

Rehearse: The Whole Body Preaches

A wonderful fact to reflect upon, that every human creature
is constituted to be that profound secret and mystery to
every other.

—Charles Dickens, *A Tale of Two Cities*

As mentioned earlier, preaching provides an opportunity to encounter Christ. The word of God mediated through the church's
minister comes alive for us in new ways. Unfortunately, a profound proclamation may be reduced to a routine explanation if
we are not properly prepared to speak it. We rehearse in order to
insure that we will preach effectively, that is to say, the proclamation will sound genuine and the congregation will receive it clearly.

The Whole Body Preaches

Preaching is an embodied exercise. It is more than a mental
activity. As the sermon moves from the mind to the mouth and
out into the ears of the congregation, we need to be concerned
with how the message moves from the preacher to the listener.
With some speakers it would seem that they are giving a completed report on what they are thinking. But if speech is a creative
act then something happens in the interaction between the speaker
and the listener. An idea is born, a heart is stirred, a lesson is
learned. Speech is a dynamic activity.

If the purpose of preaching is to teach, move, and delight, as Augustine explained, then so much more is required than simply reading a manuscript or speaking one's mind. In other words, the preacher needs to be more than a talking head. We need to ask how we will deliver the message. Here we can take another example from the dinner table. Most chefs will tell you that the presentation of a meal is a key ingredient for a good dining experience. Of course the preparation is important—but so is the presentation. The thoughtful arrangement of the food on the plate, the proper setting of the table, and the way the server carries the plate to the table will enhance the meal. The steak au poivre may be delicious to taste, but if it is served on a paper plate and placed on a greasy tablecloth, our senses may be dulled and the enjoyment lost.

Speech is like a meal, and presentation plays a key role in communicating our message. The way we speak will influence what is heard. Indeed, according to Myron Chartier, in his book *Preaching as Communication*, more is communicated through the preacher's tone of voice, bodily gestures, and facial expression than through the spoken words. So while the insights into Scripture and the well-crafted phrases are necessary, they are not sufficient. The way we present the message will affect how it will be received. Let us look at these bodily aspects of public speaking.

In rehearsing to preach there are several components to consider and we can divide them into two categories, physical and vocal. The physical includes eye contact, facial expression, and hand gestures. The vocal concerns our tone of voice as well as the rate, volume, and pitch of our speech. We will begin with the physical components.

Eye contact is essential for effective personal communication. Weren't we all taught as children to greet someone by looking the person in the eye? Those who cannot look us in the eye may seem suspicious or untrustworthy. Good eye contact helps to establish trust between people. It is the same for speaking in public.

Now, obviously a speaker cannot look at each person all the time, although some do try. Beware of two distracting moves. First, avoid "panning" the audience, that is, continuously moving the head from right to left. This could make both preacher and listener dizzy. It is more effective to look in one direction for a short time. For example, look to the right section for twenty to thirty seconds, then to the middle, and then to the left. In between shifting from one section to the next, the preacher may look down to read from the text. Second, while reading from the text, beware of "bobbing" up and down. It may show the preacher's desire to communicate directly with the congregation, but the repetitive movement of the head also may become a distraction. It is more effective to balance the reading of the text with looking out at the congregation. It helps to be familiar with the text so that we can look up without fear of losing the place on the page.

Experienced speakers learn how to format the text in a way that is easy to read. Take a lesson from the Lectionary. As we mentioned earlier, note the "sense lines" and how the Bible passages are typed in lines that express a clear thought. For example, look at the format for the first four lines of the gospel passage for Easter Sunday (John 20:1-9).

> On the first day of the week,
>> Mary of Magdala came to the tomb early in the morning,
>> while it was still dark,
>> and saw the stone removed from the tomb.

This format allows the eye to look down quickly, grasp a line, and then look up. This scheme also allows the reader to find his place again, easily. The font type can be enlarged, as well, to make for easy reading. So, instead of writing out the homily as if it were an essay, formatting with sense lines and large font lightens the burden of presentation and facilitates greater eye contact.

Eye contact may be enhanced by the speaker's facial expression. We may ask, does the expression of the preacher's face convey the emotion of the message? If you say the word "joy," it would help to look joyful. If you say "sorrow," we should see a hint of sorrow. To be sure, this is not about acting, as if we were onstage, but it will be distracting to see a disconnect between the spoken word and the facial expression. It is a matter of establishing credibility between speaker and listener. If we welcome the faithful to the "joyful Easter celebration," shouldn't we look joyful? The proper facial expression will enhance communication.

So too will our gestures. The key to the proper use of hand gestures is to employ them like our words, using them deliberately and sparingly. Some excited speakers may let their hands fly all around them in meaningless gestures. Instead we should choose gestures like words, using them to enhance the message. Also, the movement of the gesture should precede the speaking of the word. For example, think of how you would greet someone. You probably extend your hand in friendship and smile before saying the word "welcome." So, when preaching, if you are to refer to "heaven" and mean to point upwards, the pointing should precede the word by a fraction of a second.

Again, our premise is that the whole body preaches. Accordingly, it is good to remember that the ear follows the eye. This is to say that what we see will influence what we hear. (Remember the old saying, "A picture is worth a thousand words.") So it is important that our actions are consistent with our words. Some of the congregation may focus more on the gesture than on the word. I learned this the hard way. As a newly ordained priest I was speaking to a group of "young adults." They were mostly professionals, ranging in age from twenty-five to thirty-five. At the time I was in their age group. (I have come to appreciate since then that we are probably more self-conscious and more nervous in front of our peers than with any other audience. And that day I was very nervous.) This presentation of mine was the beginning of a retreat weekend and I wanted to encourage the retreatants to relax. On a retreat it is important to relax, to leave behind the stress of the daily routine and allow the word of God to speak to us. ("Be still and know that I am God.") Unfortunately, the nervousness took control of my body, and my right hand folded into a fist. Meanwhile I spoke to the group about the spiritual and personal need to relax. Afterwards a retreatant approached me. She seemed rather upset and she blurted out, "Father, did you know that you gave that whole talk on relaxation with a clenched fist?" I was not aware of it until she mentioned it. I could have talked all night long about the rewards of relaxation, but she focused on my clenched fist, which suggests anything but "relax." Yes, the ear follows the eye.

Let's digress for a moment while we are on the subject of nervousness. Why do we feel so nervous standing before an audience? What is it about standing before a group of people that strikes fear in us? Some time ago *Reader's Digest* conducted a survey of the greatest fears of their readers. The survey concluded with a list of three. The fear of flying was the third greatest fear. Second in the list was the fear of death. And the greatest fear of all was speaking in public.

An incident in high school taught me something about the fear of public speaking. I was a junior and had to give an oral presentation for my US history class. I stood before the class of twenty-five students, extremely nervous, tightly holding several index cards. I felt intimidated, presuming that they were all against me, silently sitting in judgment and criticizing me. Would they really be interested in my brief report on the Dred Scott decision? I was well prepared yet very scared. Now, right in front of me sat Mason, the cool kid in the class. Mason was not very interested in the class, or school for that matter, and appeared older than the rest of us; he was probably repeating the course. We sat in alphabetical order, which is the only reason he would be up front. So there I stood: me against the class, giving my presentation. In shuffling my cards, one fell to the floor. I froze, too nervous to pick it up. Just keep talking, I thought. But then, from the corner of my eye, I could see Mason reaching down. He picked up the card and handed it to me. I took it and thanked him, and continued talking. I felt some of the nervousness leave me. In that moment I thought that maybe some of the students were on my side, supporting me and interested in my topic. This guy would not let me sink. After class I thanked him and he replied in a friendly tone of voice, "I thought you would need it." It made me think about why I presume the audience is out to get me and why I often find myself fighting the audience, struggling to convey my point and to hold their attention. Where does this fear come from?

The fear of standing in front of a live audience to deliver a speech may strike a primal fear within us. In her book *Quiet*, Susan Cain explains that the problem may be rooted in our genes. For our ancient ancestors living on the savanna, when they were being watched intently it could only mean one thing: that they were being stalked by wild animals. And when we are being stalked and afraid of being eaten, the natural reaction is not to stand tall with a confident pose, but to get away from there as quickly as possible. As Cain says, "Hundreds of thousands of years of evolution urge us to get the hell off the stage, where we can mistake the gaze of the spectators for the glint in a predator's eye."[1] She goes on to belie the advice of picturing the audience naked. (Personally I always thought that a bit bizarre, if not disturbing in its own way.) But if the audience is imagined, through some genetic disposition, as a pride of lions on the savanna, well, the lions are already naked, so that will not help much.

So part of the fear of public speaking is that, subconsciously, we imagine that the audience intends to harm us. Their steely expression or blank stares, their fidgeting in their seats, watching their watches, or reading their smartphones all seem to growl at us. If we are hardwired to think that they are out to get us, then we will interpret any movement as a prelude to an attack. It brings us back to the question, Where do you stand with the congregation? Do you stand above them, as if you were a self-appointed authority, speaking down to the congregation? Do you stand against them, competing with them, hoping to prove you are better or smarter than they are? Or do you accompany them, standing with them, grateful for the opportunity to speak to them, and through this opportunity you will grow in understanding your own message and deepen your faith? Where we stand with the congregation will either exaggerate or ameliorate our fear of speaking in public.

However, a certain amount of fear is helpful. This fear is felt in nervous energy. There are many stories of accomplished actors who feared the stage but learned to channel that energy. They tell of the great British actor Richard Burton, who said that the day he was no longer afraid to go onstage, he would not go onstage. The actress Mary Martin, before walking onstage, is said to have stood behind the curtain and peeked out and whispered to the audience, "I love you." It was a way of helping her to focus on her purpose onstage and cast herself in the relationship of actor and audience. Or take the great preacher Walter Burghardt. In his book *Preaching: The Art and the Craft*, he describes the feeling of butterflies in his stomach before preaching. Indeed, I can remember a time, standing and talking with him shortly before he would be called to the stage to deliver a keynote speech, and he was visibly nervous. He politely excused himself and asked me to say a prayer for him. Me . . . pray for the great Fr. Burghardt?! He then went on to deliver a rousing keynote address. Yes, a certain amount of fear is good for the speaker.

Nervousness is a form of energy that we can harness to help us to be more alert to our purpose and aware of our audience. It can help us to project our voice and be more dramatic with our gestures. If we fail to harness the nervousness, it will overwhelm us. The voice will tremble, the hands will shake, we will pace back and forth, and we may lose contact with the audience. So a dose of fear is good and we must learn how to channel it.

Finally, we should return to our theme of preparation. For if we are not sure of what we intend to say, the beasts on the savanna will appear angrier and hungrier. But for the speaker who is well prepared and has a worthy message, the beasts are transformed into friends. They support and carry the speaker along. Here too there is an energy force that enlivens and encourages the speaker. Their eye contact, the slight nodding of the head, the occasional smile or laugh—all this tells the preacher that he is connecting with the audience. The speaker is energized. However, when the congregation is unresponsive, it is as if the speaker is left to carry the speech alone. It becomes tiring and burdensome.

While we are on the subject of the speaker's burden, we should consider the reality of a boring congregation. We often hear about boring preachers—and there are some. They fail to engage the congregation, who then drift off into a daydream or planning the day. However, we need to consider also that some congregations, sad to say, are boring. They fail to respond to the preacher. We will find this when too many people sitting in the pews appear disinterested. Someone picks up the parish bulletin as soon as the preaching begins. Another looks at her iPhone. They show no interest whatsoever in the preaching moment. After Mass, the people offer little or no feedback, leaving the preacher to wonder if his message came through. (Is anyone listening?) A nonresponsive congregation drains a preacher's energy and enthusiasm.

We can learn a lesson from the African-American congregation with its dynamic of "call-and-response." We are all familiar with the exchange when the preacher makes a statement and then he hears, "Amen" or "That's right." These responses let the preacher know that he is being heard and they encourage him to continue. As one pastor explained, "Here, they take it from you!" The people call the sermon out of the preacher. He needs to be prepared, of course, but in the process of preaching, the sermon comes alive. More than words on paper, this is the living word of God.

Furthermore, one way to promote interest and fend off boredom is to have the congregation come prepared by reading the Scripture before the liturgy. Some parishes list the readings for the following Sunday in the bulletin for the people to read ahead. Reflections on these Scripture passages are available also in monthly missalettes and weekly magazines. The USCCB has produced a website that lists the daily readings for a three-month period. This site provides the Scripture text for each day along with a video reflection.

Reading the Scriptures and reflecting upon them promotes interest in the preacher's message. For a long-range approach, the parish, as a whole, could be encouraged to read the gospel of the current liturgical cycle, Year A, B, or C, to have an overview of the story for the year. One preacher lightheartedly assigns "homework" in his homily, suggesting that the congregation read ahead for the following week . . . and some actually do it! After Mass some people would like to read the homily. For this, some parishes provide a copy of the homily, either on paper or on the parish website. Parishioners will use it for their personal prayer or as a way to stay connected while they are away from home.

Now let us turn to the second category concerning the preacher's body—the voice. First of all, it is important to find the appropriate tone of voice. Consider how one would preach for an infant baptism, or a wedding, or a funeral, as well as on any given Sunday. The preacher's tone of voice should help to express the joy of baptizing a baby, the excitement of a wedding, or the solemnity of a funeral. The preacher's voice carries the message.

Practically speaking, it helps to modulate one's voice lest the tone become monotonous. We modulate our speech through the volume, pitch, and rate of how we speak. Think of the voice as a musical instrument. A speaker should vary the volume, growing loud or soft when appropriate. Sometimes a point can be stressed by lowering the voice, which draws in the listeners. The speaker also varies the pitch from high to low. Listen to the trained British actors who use the whole range of their voices. There is a musical quality to their speech, which carries the audience along. Notice too that when performed well, the focus is on the words rather than on the actor. In contrast, monotonous speakers leave us fixated on their dullness until we drift into a daydream.

The rate at which we speak—fast or slow—can also be varied. The key word here is "varied." We should beware of falling into any pattern of speech since that too becomes predictable and monotonous. Also, thinking in terms of comprehension, a lighthearted comment may be said quickly and the listeners will understand the meaning. However, a point that is "heavy" or complex should be spoken slowly. For example, when explaining a technical term (like "consubstantial"), or a teaching of the church, or when stating the main point of the homily, slow speech will be effective. Moreover, pausing can be powerful. The pause in public speech serves as punctuation. It is the period or the comma in a spoken sentence. The pause can be a means of preparing the listeners for something important, or to allow them to reflect briefly on the point just made. Pausing plays a key role in the rhythm of speech.

Finding Your Voice

Finding your voice is a matter of speaking in a way that is natural for you. Some tend to speak with a "preacher's voice," putting on an air of faux sophistication. (After a year of preaching, my younger brother commented, "Your preaching sounds better. You sound less British." I was not aware that I had been falling into a British accent.) Others may try to sound terribly folksy, as a way to relate to the listeners, but they end up talking down to people.

It is important to find your own voice, that is, to speak in a way that sounds sincere. Remember Miles Davis's comment that it takes a long time to develop one's own voice. I remember a young Vietnamese deacon who worked in a parish somewhere in the suburbs of Southern California. The small congregation was filled with blond-haired, blue-eyed folks, young and old, looking like a photo on an old Beach Boys album. Meanwhile, this deacon had been very impressed by the black style of preaching that he had experienced recently in an urban parish, and he tried to copy that style. So what we heard on any given Sunday was a black preaching style in a lily-white congregation from a man with a pronounced Vietnamese accent. It was a bit of culture shock.

It takes time to find your voice, one that is comfortable for the preacher and believable to the listeners. In rehearsing, it is good to ask, Does this sound like me? Is this my normal tone of voice? Would I use these words in normal conversation? You could also ask, If I were to compare my preaching style with a style of music, which would I choose? Allow me to suggest three styles of music: classical, popular, or jazz. Now, each one of these styles is good. For preaching, the classical style calls for a well-prepared manuscript, like a conductor's score. This script will be read verbatim from the ambo. The message has a rhythm and flow, emphasizing the key points with the full range of the voice. Usually it is used for more formal occasions such as funerals, weddings, confirmations, and baccalaureate liturgies. The popular style is appropriate for less formal occasions, like daily Mass, the mother's club communion breakfast, liturgy with children or within a senior citizen residence. It will convey a clear and lively theme supported by a refrain that is easy to remember. The jazz homily falls somewhere in between these two. In this case, the preacher has a well-prepared homily with a clear theme, and it is well structured with a beginning, a middle, and an end. However, the preacher is open to how the Spirit may move through the preaching, and how the congregation may respond. For example, sometimes the preacher notices that the listeners are moved by a particular point in the homily. They appear amused, enthused, or confused. The preacher did not plan for this. But it may be an invitation to delve more deeply into that point, repeating it, rephrasing it, elaborating upon it, perhaps providing an illustration if one readily comes to mind. The preacher may develop the point without belaboring it. Then, when sensing that the congregation has been satisfied, the preacher returns to the text. All the while the preacher and congregation move together. The jazz style of preaching can be useful in a retreat setting, when the preacher and retreatants already have established a rapport, and the preacher can freely respond to the people.

In the discussion of rehearsing the homily we see that there is a performative element to preaching. The preacher must bring some skills from the stage into the pulpit. These skills and techniques help the preacher to convey the word of the Lord more effectively. However, to be clear, while we talk of a performative element, good preachers do not call attention to themselves. It is similar to the way that good storytellers keep the focus on the characters and on the narrative, rather than on themselves. Likewise, an actor onstage loses herself in the character she portrays. We do not notice the actor so much as the character. For example, when Helen Mirren plays the role of Queen Elizabeth in her masterful stage performance in *The Audience*, the theater audience soon forgets that they are watching Ms. Mirren. Rather they are engaged by the queen herself. Storytellers, actors, and preachers bring the audience into the world of the story.

In a way the preacher acts like an icon. In another book, *Living Beauty: The Art of Liturgy*, I compared the presider at liturgy to an icon. The same can be said for the preacher. Picture an icon. Icons differ from traditional paintings in that they are deliberately non-representational, that is to say, the characters are not intended to look like the people they portray. Rather they provide a suggestion of how the saints or the savior appeared. Also, icons are two-dimensional rather than three-dimensional drawings. Further, icons show no shadows, indicating that the source of light comes from behind the painting. In a sense we do not look "at" an icon so much as we look "through" it to the divine. An icon is a portal to the realm of the divine. The preacher acts like an icon in that the congregation should not notice him so much but have an opportunity to encounter the Son of God, about whom he preaches. To state it bluntly, the preacher should get out of the way of the message and let the light of Christ shine through. The well-prepared preacher stands before the church like an icon. Practicing proper preparation allows the light of Christ to shine through the preacher and the word of God to ring through the preacher's voice.

Hopefully the method proposed here will serve to lighten the burden for the preacher, rather than adding to an already busy schedule. By taking time to reflect, research, write, and rehearse, the preacher engages the Scripture both personally and pastorally, and prepares to meet the people who long to see the face of God.

PART III

Preaching for Funerals and Weddings

Our discussion of preaching has been focused on the Sunday Liturgy of the Eucharist. In the next two sections we will look at preaching for specific liturgical occasions, namely funerals and weddings. I have selected these two because they are the ones requested most by clergy in workshops on preaching.

Before launching into this discussion, though, let us add one more description for the purpose of preaching. Fred Craddock, who was mentioned earlier, said that effective preaching strives to tell people what they want to say. Note a distinction here. It is not that the preacher tells people what they want to "hear," but what they would like to say. Especially in these sacramental occasions, the preacher helps to give voice to the joys and hopes, the fear and concern of the people gathered for worship. Recalling the prophet Isaiah, the Lord has given the preacher a well-trained tongue to speak a word to rouse the people in faith. Through time spent in prayer, study of the Scripture and the tradition, and experience with the people of God, the preacher is able to name grace and announce the presence of God in the midst of the assembly. So, within the context of our faith, when preparing to preach for a funeral or a wedding, the preacher should ask, "What do the people of God want to say?"

CHAPTER NINE

The Funeral

I will be confident. . . .
I believe that I shall see the goodness of the LORD
  in the land of the living.

                                        —Psalm 27:3, 13

We begin the discussion of funeral preaching with a story. The film *Taking Chance* depicts the return of twenty-year-old Lance Corporal Chance Phelps. He was killed in combat in Iraq in 2004, on Good Friday. From this film we learn of a military custom of how the remains of a fallen marine are returned to his hometown. The casket is escorted by another marine, Lt. Col. Michael Strobl, who insures that it is shown proper respect along the way. This story is taken from the journal kept by Strobl. Before the journey begins, we see Cpl. Chance's remains treated with great care. His uniform is pressed, his military medals shined, his St. Christopher medal polished, and his watch cleaned—all this attention to detail even though the casket will remain closed during the funeral. I was reminded of the instruction from the funeral rite, "Since in baptism the body was marked with the seal of the Trinity and became the temple of the Holy Spirit, Christians respect and honor the bodies of the dead" (General Introduction 19).

The story carries neither an anti-war nor a pro-war message, but portrays an example of human dignity. The film is "Catholic" in its symbolism and sensitivity. In one moment, we see Col. Strobl seated on a commercial airplane. The coffin carrying Cpl. Chance rests in the hold of the airplane. Before take-off, a stewardess, who was moved by knowing that the plane is carrying a fallen marine, hands Col. Strobl a silver crucifix as a gift to carry with him. Also, all along the way, the coffin is handled with great care and dignity. Upon landing, when the coffin slides out of the airplane along a conveyer belt, Col. Strobl stands at full attention and salutes. When does an officer salute an enlisted man or woman? It may remind us of the early church, when the martyrs and confessors—those who suffered for the Christian faith—were held in highest esteem by the faithful.

The funeral service for Cpl. Chance is held in a school gymnasium, which is probably the only space in town that could hold the large gathering. It is unfortunate for our purposes that the sermon is omitted. Perhaps we could say that the whole story is the sermon. Nevertheless, the purpose of preaching, as explained earlier, is not simply to embellish the liturgy with one more element, but to help us interpret the event. Preaching opens the experience of worship so that we may better understand its effect on us, and what difference it makes in our lives. Preaching promotes a conversion of hearts and minds so that we might understand our relationship with the Lord in a new way. This film helps to change our perspective on life and death, fostering a new appreciation for human life.

Here is the instruction for preaching a funeral, quoted in full, as taken from the *Order of Christian Funerals* (141):

> A brief homily based on the readings should always be given at the funeral liturgy, but never any kind of eulogy. The homilist should dwell on God's compassionate love and on the paschal mystery of the Lord as proclaimed in the Scripture readings. Through the homily, the community should receive the consolation and strength to face the death of one of its members with a hope that has been nourished by the proclamation of the saving word of God.

Let's look at the key points of this instruction. First, the funeral homily should be rooted in the Scripture proclaimed at the liturgy. The ritual book for the funeral contains many suggestions for readings from the Old Testament and New Testament, the psalms, and the gospels. The instruction also makes clear that the preaching should be a homily and not a eulogy, that is, it should not be an oration in praise of a person. The funeral is not so much about the person's life itself, but more about how God has been manifested through this person's life. Moreover, it is the occasion to reaffirm our faith in the paschal mystery of Jesus Christ. The funeral forces us to confront the crux of our faith: that Jesus, the Lord, died and rose again to new life. And the Lord holds out this same promise to us: we will rise again after death. Here, in a sound bite, we have the paschal mystery. The funeral can pose a challenge to a preacher's faith: Do I really believe that Jesus Christ is the Son of God, who suffered and died for the redemption of human sinfulness, and rose again to be with the Father in glory forever, and that we share in this promise of everlasting life? Do we believe this and do we have the conviction to proclaim it?

Never a Eulogy

Many funeral homilies skirt the issue of the paschal mystery; instead they devolve into a eulogy. It is less challenging to extoll the virtues of the deceased, sprinkled with several lighthearted anecdotes. Once again we need to ask, Whose story will the congregation remember—the story of the Lord or of the deceased? The preacher's eulogy is like a fast-food meal: pleasant tasting and filling, but later we are left with little spiritual nutrition. To be sure, we should talk about the deceased with an emphasis on how this person's life helped to illuminate the presence of Christ in the lives of those who knew him or her.

As an aside, we should say a word about the eulogy in general. Many dioceses in the United States forbid eulogies given by family or friends during the liturgy. This is wise. In too many cases these eulogies have made for embarrassing moments. Consider that most people today are not trained for public speaking. At a funeral, which is often an emotionally charged situation, the eulogist will try to express his or her sentiment before a crowd of family, friends, and strangers. This is no time for a lesson in oratory. Too many speakers, thinking that they knew what they wanted to say before they stood before the audience, drift along, searching for the right words and images, and they drone on for a long time. Some even slip into vulgarity, hoping to convey emotion. As a rule, then, eulogies should be delivered at the vigil, which is usually a setting that is less formal and more relaxed, and more conducive for storytelling.

Besides this, a bad eulogy may disrupt the flow of the funeral liturgy. Consider that the liturgy begins with heightened emotion. The gathering of the mourners around the casket in the vestibule of the church signals finality. The night before, at the vigil, we told our stories and remembered the deceased as a vibrant, perhaps quirky, person. This morning we come to bid farewell to our loved one and friend. During the liturgy we move forward. The Scripture readings, the homily, and the eucharistic prayer help to move us, pointing the direction from this life to eternal life. For example, in the "final commendation" the priest says, "One day we shall joyfully greet him/her again when the love of Christ, which conquers all things, destroys even death itself" (Invitation to Prayer 171A). The point is that the funeral liturgy helps to carry us along through our grief with the hope of eternal rest. However, the eulogy, when delivered after Communion, with a grief-stricken message, may disrupt the flow of the liturgy.

The Challenge of Funeral Preaching

Preaching for a funeral entails a host of problems. For example, the preacher has to contend with the funeral industry, a rapidly rising conglomerate. The buzzword for funeral home advertising is to "personalize" the occasion. The family and friends of the deceased are encouraged to send their loved ones off in style, emphasizing their unique lifestyles. Here is an example of the commodification of our sacramental celebrations. The ceremonies of the Catholic Church have entered the marketplace where companies influence how we celebrate. This is especially true for funerals and weddings.

One question I was asked repeatedly while in Australia was what I thought about using a PowerPoint presentation during a funeral Mass. This presentation flashes pictures of the deceased onto a screen that has been set up in the sanctuary. (In Australia, many parishes already have screens in the sanctuary and they are used for the Sunday liturgy. The hymns are projected onto the screen, which serves as a hymnal and avoids the cost of purchasing many books and shipping them overseas.) One concern with these presentations is that the focus of our attention may fall on the deceased alone rather than on the paschal mystery.

The preacher must also contend with some unique issues when preparing for a funeral. For instance, sometimes there is very little time for preparation. This is true especially in the case of a tragic death, when emotions will run high and questions abound, as we try to make sense of an accident or an act of violence. This points to another challenge for funeral preaching: trying to find meaning when faced with tragedy. Preachers rely on their knowledge of the Scripture and of the church's teaching, and they seek to apply this tradition to the present situation. Being rational creatures, we human beings need to make sense of our lives. We believe that everything has a purpose. And sometimes we will invent a purpose in order to satisfy our curiosity. We have all heard the pious bromides such as "God works in mysterious ways." These are offered to salve a suffering soul. For example, at the wake of a five-year-old girl, someone tried to console the little girl's mother by explaining that "God loved her so much that he wanted her back with him." The grieving mother replied, "Well, then, to hell with God!" I am inclined to think that God agreed with the mother. Do we really believe that God snatches people away from their loving families for his personal pleasure? What is our image of God?

I remember a personal experience. My cousin, Jeanette, was one of the more than three thousand victims in New York City on September 11, 2001. Our family held a memorial service in her home parish in Brooklyn, New York. After the service I greeted her friends who came from around the city to mourn and to pay their respects. One of her friends blurted out in her sadness, "She was a hero. She died for her country." I listened politely and thanked her for coming to the service. Now, this was not the time or place to disagree with her. But what I wanted to say was that, sadly, my cousin was not a hero and she did not die for her country. She never had the chance to do so. On the contrary, she died an innocent victim. However, in our striving to make sense we sometimes fabricate meaning. The preacher should not try to explain why such a tragedy occurred, because sometimes there is no explanation. The preacher will remind us of where we have come from with the Lord, and point the way to where we go from here, trusting in the mercy of God. Again, we are hopeful, rather than merely optimistic.

One other challenge for the preacher at a funeral is having to face a diverse congregation. Sitting in the benches before us we find the devout alongside the deserters, that is, those who attend church regularly and those who have fallen away, due to either protest or lethargy. Then there are those who worship with other denominations and faiths, as well as the atheists and the "nones." And the preacher is supposed to have a word for all of the assembly. The preacher will confront the temptation to water down the message to make it palatable for the masses. Here we may find the subtle urge to turn the funeral homily into a eulogy. However, the Christian teaching offers a richer fare for all. The belief in eternal life holds out hope for all people. This belief is universal and historical, shared by people throughout the world and through all time. Christians are empowered in their belief by the story of Jesus Christ, and this message is truly universal.

Furthermore, the instruction for funeral preaching calls for compassion and consolation to be shown to those who are grieving. This compassion is displayed throughout the liturgy when the coffin is brought to the church and carried inside with dignity, when it is incensed and sprinkled with holy water. The care for the body of the deceased displays respect for all who are gathered. It is a reminder of the dignity that should be shown to all human beings.

At this point we should note how the symbols of baptism reappear in the funeral liturgy. The sprinkling reminds us of the baptismal bath that washed away the effects of original sin and welcomed us into the Christian community. The light of the paschal candle reminds us of the candle that was lit for us at baptism as a light to guide us along the way toward salvation. And the funeral pall—the white cloth covering the coffin—reminds us of the white garment we donned at our baptism, a sign that we became a new person in Jesus Christ. The prayer of the funeral rite rings clearly here: "In baptism N. received the light of Christ. Scatter the darkness now and lead him/her over the waters of death" (General Intercessions 167A).

As an even more effective sign, some modern churches have constructed a baptismal pool at the entranceway. The position of the pool signifies that the way we enter the church community is through baptism. The sacrament is celebrated in a dramatic way with the person descending into the pool, being washed, and then stepping out and walking into the church. The movement symbolizes dying to oneself and rising with Christ. Then, for the funeral rite, the pool is covered with a metal grate. The coffin is processed into the church and placed on the grate, making a visual connection between baptism and the promise of eternal life.

Finally, the funeral liturgy is actually a movement in three parts: the vigil service, the funeral liturgy, and the burial. We move from the funeral home, to the church, and then to the cemetery. For our Christian ancestors, worship was seldom stationary but always celebrated "on the move." The movement indicated the journey of faith for "the way," as the early Christians were called. They were indeed a "pilgrim church." The funeral procession commenced at the house of the deceased with prayer. Then the company of mourners escorted the body and the grieving family to the church. And as they walked they chanted. At the church they celebrated a liturgy expressing their faith in the paschal mystery and their hope in everlasting life with Christ. From the church they processed to the burial site, again chanting along the way. Finally, at the cemetery they committed the deceased to the ground, entrusting the person to the eternal care of God. Perhaps an explanation of this tradition will inspire some in their longing to see the Lord in the land of the living.

CHAPTER TEN

The Wedding

What is a friend? A single soul dwelling in two bodies.

—Aristotle

Preaching for a wedding is yet another illustration of the mantra, "Preaching is difficult." Most priests and deacons I talk with say that they would prefer to celebrate a funeral more than a wedding. Why is that? Does it have something to do with the wedding industry and its focus on the "bride's day"? We will address this shortly.

Let us begin by reviewing the instruction for the marriage homily. This is taken from the Order of Celebrating Matrimony Within Mass (57):

> After the reading of the Gospel, the Priest in the Homily uses the sacred text to expound the mystery of Christian Marriage, the dignity of conjugal love, the grace of the Sacrament, and the responsibilities of married people, keeping in mind, however, the various circumstances of individuals.

To this we might add lightheartedly, "and all of this in eight minutes!" Clearly this is a lot to handle. Let's focus on the last point, "keeping in mind, however, the various circumstances of individuals." We can presume that these circumstances include the makeup of the congregation. Imagine the variety of people gathered in this assembly. It will surpass St. Gregory's thirty-six

pairs of opposites, mentioned earlier. Joining us in this congregation are those who are happily married as well as some who are
divorced; widows and widowers; those wishing to be married
and those wondering why they remain married; those dreaming
of finding the right partner and those simply waiting for the reception. The wedding, like the funeral, will also bring together
people of different faiths, the nonbelievers, and the disaffected.

Moreover, like the funeral, the wedding ceremony has been
commodified by a commercial industry, and has even been made
a farce. A quick review of popular films that deal with marriage
shows the wedding to be frivolous. For example, look at *Mamma
Mia!*, *Bride Wars*, and *Four Weddings and a Funeral*. In this last film,
the four weddings are laughable, while the funeral is treated with
reverence. The wedding industry focuses on the wedding ceremony, promising to make this the most wonderful day in the life
of the couple. To be precise, it is treated as the bride's day.

The average cost for this big day was $32,641 in 2015, not in-
cluding the honeymoon.[1] With so much emphasis on the big day,
there is little concern for the marriage itself. Catholic Engaged
Encounter reminds the engaged couples during a weekend retreat,
"A wedding is a day but a marriage is a lifetime." The wedding
industry has actually put up obstacles for some couples. Some
have admitted that while they would really like to marry, they are
deterred by the expectation of an elaborate ceremony and reception. Today's weddings carry a huge price tag, both financially
and emotionally. However, those who are considering marriage
need to know that it does not have to be this way. A ceremony,
simple but elegant, followed by a gathering of family and friends,
is all that is required for a faithful and festive celebration. To be
sure, there is nothing wrong with an elaborate reception within
the financial means of the families, but it seems a shame that this
has become the expectation for American weddings.

Also, similar to the preaching for a funeral, at a wedding we
sometimes hear a "eulogy" instead of a homily. The preacher needs
to focus on the covenant of marriage more than on the couple. It
is the Christian understanding of covenant that makes marriage
a sacrament for Catholics. But when the preacher focuses so much
on the couple, the homily will sound like a eulogy, in the literal

meaning of the word, that is, a speech in praise of a person. In the wedding eulogy, the preacher will praise the couple, pointing out how lovely they look together, how long he has known the bride or groom or both, and commenting on their future together. Some preachers feel compelled to reveal pieces of information they know about the couple in hopes of establishing credibility with the congregation or simply to get a laugh. But this sort of eulogy is part of the hype that plays into the hands of the wedding industry—the hype that sells the wedding day as the most important day of a woman's life.

Here's a shock: I tell the couple as they are preparing their wedding, that the wedding is not about them. Rather, we celebrate what God is doing through this man and woman. By comparison, the ordination day is not about the newly ordained priest. I can remember a day shortly before my ordination. Standing in the recreation room of the Jesuit community, I was talking about the plans for my first Mass, "The Mass of Thanksgiving," in my home parish. I must have sounded like a nervous groom before the wedding day. One of the older and wiser fathers spoke up from across the room: "Just remember, Tom, you're the occasion for the party, not the attraction." It was a salient and sobering point, and well taken. The purpose of sacramental celebration is not so much to celebrate an individual, but to provide a sign of God's presence among us. Here is an opportunity to encounter God.

In marriage, the Christian community gains a glimpse of God's love for humanity. In the statement of promises made by the bride and groom, we learn something about God's great love for us. The couple proclaims and promises, "I take you to be my wife/husband. I promise to be faithful to you, in good times and in bad, in sickness and in health, to love you and to honor you all the days of my life." Here human speech manifests God's love. (Once again, words matter.) In hearing these promises we are reminded how God chose us. Jesus said, "You did not choose me but I chose you. And I appointed you to go and bear fruit, fruit that will last, so that the Father will give you whatever you ask him in my name" (John 15:16). God promised to care for his people and to be true to them for all eternity. In turn God asked for fidelity from his chosen people. In the dialogue spoken by the bride and groom, we hear this promise and response played out once again.

Here is the covenant of marriage. Two people enter into an agreement fully, freely, and forever. Both enter into marriage in freedom, as they respond to the first question asked by the minister, "Have you come here to enter into Marriage without coercion, freely and wholeheartedly?" They enter into this covenant fully, that is to say, unconditionally, with no strings attached, promising to savor the joy, and struggle with sorrow, together. And they enter into this life forever. Their intention is to grow old together, remaining with each other, living out their vocation for the rest of their lives. In Jesus' words, "A man shall leave his father and mother and be joined to his wife, and the two shall become one flesh" (Mark 10:6-8).

This covenant differs from a legal contract. To explain the difference simply, a contract is an agreement between two parties that requires a quid pro quo (this for that). The party of the first part will do X for the party of the second part, and the second party promises to do Y in return. This is the basis of a simple contract. But the Christian covenant goes beyond the contract in that both parties make a promise to each other and will abide by it even when it is difficult or impossible for the other to respond. For example, in the film *Still Alice*, it is moving to see how, after Alice is struck with Alzheimer's disease, her husband cares for her so lovingly. He gives us an example of a spouse remaining faithful "in sickness and in health." Even though it is impossible for Alice to respond to her husband, he maintains his promise, caring for his wife.

God promised to care for the Israelites of old, and to love them and to see them succeed as a great nation. And God asked for their fidelity in return. However, even when Israel turned away from the Lord, even when they were unfaithful, God remained true to them. For example, hear the word of God as spoken through the prophet Hosea: "How can I give you up, Ephraim? / How can I hand you over, O Israel? . . . My heart recoils within me; / my compassion grows warm and tender. / I will not execute my fierce anger . . . for I am God and no mortal, / the Holy One in your midst" (Hos 11:8-9). The story of the divine covenant is reflected in the marriage vows.

Can Anyone Say "Forever"?

Within modern society another question looms. How can anyone say "forever"? Is it reasonable to make such a promise in our day? Consider that, today, people in the Western world live much longer than they did up until the twentieth century. Before 1900, the average life expectancy was forty-eight years of age. Today Americans are expected to live to the age of seventy-nine, not ignoring the many octogenarians and nonagenarians we know. Today, "forever" lasts much longer than it did for previous generations.

Consider also that in a culture marked by individualism, there is much emphasis placed on personal satisfaction and instant gratification. The idea of committing one's life to another person, forever, seems to rub against the grain of freedom and self-fulfillment. I can remember a discussion with several engaged couples. One woman voiced her concern that she was afraid that she might lose her individuality in marriage. Now, certainly this can be a problem for some married people. One spouse becomes known as the wife or husband of the other, and may come to think that she or he has no personal identity. Clearly, marriage is not for everyone. However, could it also be true that, in giving oneself to another in a relationship of lasting love, one's identity will be renewed and enriched? Christian marriage poses a paradox: In giving one's life to another, one receives much more in return. The lesson of marriage echoes this well-known gospel passage: "For those who want to save their life will lose it, and those who lose their life for my sake will save it" (Luke 9:24; cf. Matt 10:39; 16:25; Mark 8:35). The Christian couple entering into marriage believe that, through a relationship of lasting love, they will "find themselves," that is to say, they will become the people God intended them to be.

A permanent relationship is not something to be treated lightly. It must be entered into sincerely with the intention of a sustained commitment. But would it make sense to enter into marriage in any other way? It is one thing if a couple chooses to cohabitate either for a while or forever. This is a topic for another conversation. But there are some relationships that will thrive only when lived out with the promise of "forever," that is, with the hope of a lasting commitment. The permanence of marriage and the promise of fidelity offer freedom to a young couple. It is freeing to know that your partner will be there to support you and will remain with you forever. Also, children need to know their parents will be there for them, always. There is a freedom that comes with the ability to rely upon the fidelity of others in these long-lasting relationships, and this fidelity reflects the love of God.

To be clear, in marriage we are striving for an ideal. We stand before God and the community of the church reaching for a goal that is beyond ourselves, but we are confident that we will attain it. If we believe that marriage is a vocation, then we believe that God calls a married couple into being, unites them in the covenant, and will see them through to its fulfillment. The community, witnessing the newly formed covenant, consents to accompany them, supporting them along the way. Their love, expressed through their vows, reflects the lessons about love that they have learned from family and friends throughout their lives. The public expression of their love at the wedding is a statement of gratitude to those who have brought them to this moment in time. Called by God and supported by the church, they can engage in the diligent striving for their ideal.

Similarly, as a Jesuit novice I professed first vows to my provincial and to the Society of Jesus many years ago. Kneeling in the sanctuary of the Fordham University Church, with my classmates, we read the vow formula composed by St. Ignatius of Loyola, the founder of the Society:

> Almighty and eternal God, I, Thomas Scirghi, though altogether most unworthy in Your divine sight, yet relying on Your infinite goodness and mercy and moved with a desire of serving You, in the presence of the most Holy Virgin Mary and Your whole heavenly court, vow to Your Divine Majesty perpetual poverty, chastity and obedience in the Society of Jesus, and I promise that I shall enter that same Society in order to lead my entire life in it . . .

At twenty-two years of age, and a recent college graduate, there I was, making this promise before God and the whole heavenly court, no less. It was audacious. But my classmates and I were emboldened by the following phrase, "And just as You gave me to desire and offer this, so You will also bestow abundant grace to fulfill it." By the grace of God we will succeed. One cannot enter wholeheartedly into religious life—or marriage—for a while.

Finally, an essential component of living out the covenant of marriage forever is the ability to forgive one another. Forgiveness is crucial to the stability of married love. It is said that to err is human, and to forgive is divine. The vocation of marriage becomes charged with grace when the partners learn to acknowledge the hurt and harm caused by each other, yet strive to rid themselves of anger and bitterness toward one another. The notion, made famous by the film *Love Story*, that "Love means never having to say you're sorry" is fatuous. Ask any married couple. True love means always having to say we are sorry and, with God's grace, we can expect to be forgiven.

As stated earlier, a sacramental wedding is not about the couple alone, but what God is doing through them for the good of his people. There is a message for all to hear, and that is how God loves us—freely, fully, and forever—and how we may respond to this divine gift of love.

CONCLUSION

Where Does the Preacher Stand?

To conclude our discussion, let us return to the question of the preacher's stance, that is, Where does the preacher stand in relation to the members of the congregation? To clarify this relationship, recall the story of Jesus and the paralyzed man (Luke 5:17-26). Remember how the friends of the paralyzed man carried him on a stretcher to see Jesus. Remember, too, their act of desperation when they found the house filled with people. They were not able to pass through the crowd. In their determination to bring their friend to Jesus they climbed to the roof, removed some of the tiles to create an opening, and gently lowered their friend to the floor. When Jesus saw this he marveled at the faith of these men. Interestingly we never hear from the paralyzed man himself, but the action of his friends displays great faith.

St. Luke writes, "When [Jesus] saw their faith, he said, 'Friend, your sins are forgiven.'" Now, the Pharisees in the house took offense at this, thinking it blasphemous for Jesus to claim that he could forgive a person's sins. So Jesus responded to them, "You may know that the Son of Man has authority on earth to forgive sins." Then he turned to the crippled man, and told him, "Stand up and take your bed and go to your home." And the man did so, immediately, giving praise to God as he left the house. Jesus demonstrated, once again, that God has the authority to forgive sins and to heal the sick. His action echoes the prayer of the psalmist that began this book: "The LORD's are the earth and its fullness; / the world and those who dwell in it." And the people who seek the Lord with a pure heart will receive blessings.

The preacher stands with the men who bring their friend before the Lord. As we said earlier, the preacher mediates the meeting between the Lord and his people. The preacher comes to know the Lord, borne from the fruit of prayer, and knows the people well, like a shepherd who knows his sheep.

So where does the preacher stand? Some preachers choose to stand outside the house, telling people what is going on inside the house. They talk *about* the Lord, like reporters at a news event. However, effective preachers open up the house and go inside and bring the faithful with them. They know the power and the mercy of the Lord, and they know what it is that the people seek. They are heralds of God's word. Through their preaching they declare, "Lord, this is the people that longs to see your face."

Notes

Introduction

1. Quotations from Vatican II documents are taken from Austin Flannery, ed., *Vatican Council II: Constitutions, Decrees, Declarations; The Basic Sixteen Documents* (Collegeville, MN: Liturgical Press, 2014).

PART I

1. The New Evangelization for the Transmission of the Christian Faith, *Instrumentum Laboris* (Vatican City: Libreria Editrice Vaticana, 2012), 18.

Chapter 1

1. Mary Catherine Hilkert, *Naming Grace: Preaching and the Sacramental Imagination* (New York: Continuum, 1997), 44.
2. *Catechism of the Catholic Church*, 2nd ed. (United States Catholic Conference—Libreria Editrice Vaticana, 1997), 1996–97.
3. Richard Lischer, *A Theology of Preaching: The Dynamics of the Gospel* (Eugene, OR: Wipf & Stock, 1992), 82.

Chapter 2

1. John Updike, *Rabbit Is Rich*, in *The Rabbit Novels*, vol. 2 (New York: Ballantine, 2003), 219.

Chapter 3

1. Pope Francis, Plenary Session of the Pontifical Academy of Sciences, October 27, 2014 (Libreria Editrice Vaticana).
2. Ibid.
3. Avery Dulles, *A Testimonial to Grace* (Kansas City: Sheed & Ward, 1996), 35–39.
4. Rendel Harris, trans., *The Expository Times* XVIII, no. 3 (December 1906): 98.
5. Roger Haight, *Christian Spirituality for Seekers* (Maryknoll, NY: Orbis, 2012), xx.

Chapter 4

1. Mary Catherine Hilkert, *Naming Grace: Preaching and the Sacramental Imagination* (New York: Continuum, 1997), 52.
2. US bishops, *Preaching the Mystery of Faith: The Sunday Homily* (Washington, DC: USCCB, 2012), 14.
3. Ibid., 15.
4. Colt Anderson, *Christian Eloquence: Contemporary Doctrinal Preaching* (Chicago: Hillenbrand, 2005), 220.
5. Elie Wiesel, *The Gates of the Forest*, trans. Frances Frenaye (New York: Avon Books, 1966), 6–10.

PART II

1. US bishops, *Fulfilled in Your Hearing: The Homily in the Sunday Assembly* (Washington, DC: USCCB, 1982), 29.

Chapter 5

1. Brendan Byrne, *The Hospitality of God: A Reading of Luke's Gospel* (Collegeville, MN: Liturgical Press, 2015), 27.
2. Pope Francis, Chrism Mass Homily, St. Peter's Basilica (Libreria Editrice Vaticana, 2013).
3. Richard Lischer, *Theories of Preaching: Selected Readings in the Homiletical Tradition* (Durham, NC: Labyrinth, 1987), 261–64.
4. Francis, Holy Mass with Priestly Ordinations, Vatican Basilica, April 26, 2015 (Libreria Editrice Vaticana).
5. Francis, Morning Meditation, Domus Sanctae Marthae Chapel, May 6, 2015 (Libreria Editrice Vaticana).

Chapter 7

1. US bishops, *Fulfilled in Your Hearing: The Homily in the Sunday Assembly* (Washington, DC: USCCB, 1982), 33.
2. Arthur Miller, *The Crucible* (New York: Penguin, 1976), act 1.
3. Walter Kasper, *An Introduction to Christian Faith* (London: Burns & Oates, 1980). Cited in James Martin, *Between Heaven and Mirth: Why Joy, Humor, and Laughter Are at the Heart of the Spiritual Life* (New York: HarperCollins, 2011), 143.
4. Brendan Byrne, *The Hospitality of God: A Reading of Luke's Gospel* (Collegeville, MN: Liturgical Press, 2015), 121.
5. Pope Francis, Homily, Vatican's St. Martha guesthouse, January 8, 2016. Quoted in Elise Harris, "Pope Francis: When You Say 'Love,' Do You Really Know What It Means?," *Catholic News Agency*, http://www.catholicnewsagency.com/news/pope-francis-when-you-say-love-do-you-really-know-what-it-means-55674/.
6. Leo Tolstoy, *Anna Karenina*, trans. Louise and Aylmer Maude (New York: Dover, 2004), 127.

7. Fyodor Dostoevsky, *The Brothers Karamazov*, trans. Constance Garnett (New York: W.W. Norton, 2011), 55.

Chapter 8

1. Susan Cain, *Quiet: The Power of Introverts in a World That Can't Stop Talking* (New York: Crown, 2012), 107–8.

Chapter 10

1. "Wedding Spend Reaches All-Time High as Couples Look to Make the Ultimate Personal Statement," XO Group, April 5, 2016, http://ir.xogroupinc.com/investor-relations/press-releases/press-release-details/2016/Wedding-Spend-Reaches-All-Time-High-As-Couples-Look-To-Make-The-Ultimate-Personal-Statement-According-To-The-Knot-2015-Real-Weddings-Study/default.aspx.